AGHA SH⬛⬛⬛⬛⬛⬛⬛⬛⬛⬛⬛⬛⬛⬛⬛⬛⬛⬛⬛⬛LINI
REINALD⬛⬛⬛⬛⬛⬛⬛⬛⬛⬛⬛⬛⬛⬛⬛⬛⬛⬛⬛⬛TIN
JAMES B⬛⬛⬛⬛⬛⬛⬛⬛⬛⬛⬛⬛⬛⬛⬛⬛⬛⬛⬛AM
GARY BO⬛⬛⬛⬛⬛⬛⬛⬛⬛⬛⬛⬛⬛⬛⬛⬛⬛⬛LES
JOE BRAI⬛⬛⬛⬛⬛⬛⬛⬛⬛⬛⬛⬛⬛⬛⬛⬛⬛ARD
CARPENTER CONSTANTINE CAVAFY LUIS CERNUDA A. J. CHILSON
JUSTIN CHIN PHILIP F. CLARK JEFFERY CONWAY ALFRED CORN ED COX
HART CRANE QUENTIN CRISP DAVID CUMMER GAVIN GEOFFREY DILLARD
TIM DLUGOS PATRICK DONNELLY ROBERT DUNCAN ARTHUR DURKEE JIM
ELLEDGE ROBERT FRIEND JACK FRITSCHER FEDERICO GARCÍA LORCA
KEITH GAREBIAN JEAN GENET ALEX GILDZEN ROBERT L. GIRON ALLEN
GINSBERG DAVID GROFF THOM GUNN FITZ-GREENE HALLECK NICHOLAS
ALEXANDER HAYES MARTIN HARRISON MARSDEN HARTLEY TREBOR
HEALEY ESSEX HEMPHILL GREG HEWETT SCOTT HIGHTOWER WALTER
HOLLAND GERARD MANLEY HOPKINS A. E. HOUSMAN ANDREW HOWDLE
LANGSTON HUGHES MICHAEL HYDE GEORGE K. ILSLEY CHRISTOPHER
ISHERWOOD DEREK JARMAN CURRAN JEFFERY JEE LEONG KOH EDWARD
LACEY MICHAEL LASSELL TRAVIS CHI WING LAU D. H. LAWRENCE DANIEL
W.K. LEE CHIP LIVINGSTON TIMOTHY LIU RAYMOND LUCZAK JEFF MANN
JAIME MANRIQUE HERBERT WOODWARD MARTIN MARCOS L. MARTÍNEZ J.
D. McCLATCHY CLAUDE McKAY DERMOT MEAGHER HERMAN MELVILLE
JAMES MERRILL JORY MICKELSON STEPHEN S. MILLS YUKIO MISHIMA
PAUL MONETTE MICHAEL KIESOW MOORE SP MULROY CHAEL NEEDLE
ERIC THOMAS NORRIS HAROLD NORSE FRANK O'HARA SHINOBU
ORIKUCHI WILFRED OWEN PIER PAOLO PASOLINI JAMES PENHA SETH
PENNINGTON FERNANDO PESSOA FELICE PICANO VYTAUTAS PLIURA
MARTIN POUSSON MARCEL PROUST CHRISTOPHER RECORDS WILLIAM
REICHARD DENNIS RHODES ROCCO RUSSO ASSOTTO SAINT ROBERTO F.
SANTIAGO GERARD SARNAT P. C. SCEARCE JAMES SCHUYLER JAMES
SCHWARTZ DAVIS G. SEE GREGG SHAPIRO REGINALD SHEPHERD BEN
SHIELDS ALLEN SMITH MICHAEL D. SNEDIKER FREDERICK SPEERS JACK
SPICER MALCOLM STUHLMILLER MUTSUO TAKAHASHI ATSUSUKE TANAKA
GUY TERRELL ULYSSES TETU DUNSTAN THOMPSON JOHN WHITTIER
TREAT DAVID TRINIDAD MANUEL ULACIA CLAYTON L. VALLI JACK
VEASEY PAUL VERLAINE MARK WARD EDMUND WHITE JAMES L.
WHITE JOHN WIENERS SCOTT WIGGERMAN OSCAR WILDE JONATHAN
WILLIAMS TENNESSEE WILLIAMS JIM WISE CYRIL WONG IAN YOUNG

Lovejets

queer male poets on 200 years of

Walt Whitman

raymond luczak
editor

Squares & Rebels
Minneapolis, MN

In Gratitude

Editing an anthology the size of this one is always a mammoth undertaking, so the editor has always appreciated each nugget of advice, insight, and guidance no matter how seemingly insignificant: David Cummer, Scott Holl, and Eric Thomas Norris. The editor is most grateful to Richard Blanco for his kind words. And in particular, he also thanks Austin Dacey for the use of his father Philip Dacey's poem "Walt and Joe." That remarkable poem convinced him that this project was worth doing.

Copyright

Squares & Rebels
PO Box 3941
Minneapolis, MN 55403-0941
squaresandrebels@gmail.com

Printed in the United States of America.
ISBN: 978-1-941960-13-4
Library of Congress Control Number: 2018914576

A Squares & Rebels First Edition

Lineages

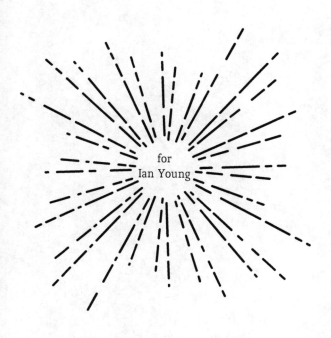

for
Ian Young

Walt and Joe

Until I learned that my father was bisexual,
I had never thought of associating him
with Walt Whitman. It had always been easier
connecting my mother to the poet—she'd have fit in
at Pfaff's, playing piano for all the revelers
as she did at parties in our apartment,
and wasn't Whitman the mother of us all?

But now I see that my father,
uneducated, a laborer, no more bookish
than the tradesmen and mechanics Whitman loved,
could have been one of his roughs—
though a gentle, sweet one—
on the Brooklyn docks.

In the picture of my father and his navy buddy,
both of them in uniform, heads close together,
I want that discoloration in the background
to be not the work of time
but the ghost of the poet,
an emanation like a blessing on these thoughts.

And because I believe that Whitman, who said
he met strangers in the street and loved them,
would have loved my father if he had met him,
I hereby take my father's hand and place it in Walt's
to introduce them: Walt, Joe; Pop, Walt.

Let them talk of mothers—
Whitman's beloved one, my orphaned father's
dead before he could remember her—
and war—the Civil and the First World wars.

And maybe my father says something of me,
how he feared my education would separate us
though it never did.

And now they are sleeping together, arms
thrown leisurely around each other,
perhaps in the bunkbed of the ship
my father sailed on, the small space
made even smaller by the presence of the two bodies,
their long peaceful breaths mingling as they dream.
That's Walt Whitman, I'd say, to anyone who'd listen and
     look,
and next to him, I'd add proudly, that's my father.

A Chain of Lineages

You know times have truly changed in the last two centuries when a heterosexual male writer—Philip Dacey, in this case—is willing to imagine his bisexual working-class father ensconced in Walt Whitman's arms in a poem filled with not a twitch of disgust but a loving pride in seeing two of his heroes sleeping together. That poem convinced me that it was indeed time to explore whether Walt Whitman and his forebears still mattered in our world, which seems so far removed from the days when gay male sexuality couldn't be discussed openly without fear of reprisal or imprisonment.

In 1855, when Walt Whitman self-published the first edition of *Leaves of Grass* by typesetting the then-untitled poems and hand-cranking the sheets that would be sliced into pages, it was a bold act of defiance. He knew he couldn't be openly gay, but it's all there, woven into the texture of his poetry. You just had to know where to look beneath the veneer of his lines. His all-encompassing vision of America and its multitudes while unafraid of death and loss shocked many readers, but gay readers still in the closet often intuited that he was family. Besides, he was among the first living writers to include a picture of himself in a book, and in workingman clothes at that, and with his hand lingering inside his pants. Respectable authors just didn't do that!

He wanted to be wanted. While doing research for my book *The Kiss of Walt Whitman Still on My Lips*, I had to chortle when I learned about a sharp-eyed straight researcher noticing how Whitman had his phallic heft enlarged in the Hollyer lithograph in the subsequent editions of *Leaves of Grass*. He wanted to get laid!

Yes, he wrote lugubrious lines that rambled on forever. Yes, most of his later work seems over-indulgent. Yes, many of his poems can feel workman-like. And yet *Leaves of Grass*, particularly the second edition published in 1856, is a masterpiece of vision expressed so clearly with no hesitation whatsoever. Suddenly we feel filled with jaw-dropping possibility. It is an unforgettable clarion call that still beckons many of us queer male poets to church. This anthology is a hymnal.

Walt Whitman wasn't the only gay poet-preacher, of course. Many others after him have lived and died in the last two centuries since he was born, leaving behind hymns that still sing in wildly different tongues to us living today. They seem to grasp, despite the eras long passed since their passing, that untranslated and unarticulated language deep inside of us. Suddenly we don't feel alone in that strange country made up of people who'd prefer that we queer men not exist.

It is doubly important to acknowledge others who've lived and left their mark on us, because if we don't, each generation of queer male poets after us will forget us long after we've returned to the earth. Let this book become a genealogy of our souls. Within these pages, all of us are family.

In that spirit, I want to spotlight Ian Young's achievements as editor and promoter of gay male poetry with his amazing anthologies *The Male Muse: A Gay Anthology* (1973) and *The Son of the Male Muse: New Gay Poetry* (1983). That Young's pivotal role in the early heady days of gay publishing, particularly in Canada, has been overlooked—or perhaps forgotten—is a real shame. His *Male Muse* anthologies have become an extraordinary reliquary of many voices no longer with us and therefore precious. They too wanted to be remembered.

When we write poetry, we want something of us to linger in the ether between our breathing and their reading, at least long enough to perfume their memories. The poets who've preceded us are multitudinous, and it is obviously impossible to go into detail about each of the poets—over 60 of them honored by over 80 living poets!—so acknowledged in these pages. Please think of each poem in this anthology as a dog-eared photograph taped into scrapbooks that get passed around at family reunions, prompting stories and introductions to relatives you didn't know you had. Seek out their work and their memories. Their voices may surprise, infuriate, and yet inspire you. Just like family.

Through Walt Whitman and his forebears, we have become a chain of lineages through the lovejets of our imaginations. May our lives and lines forever explode like the stars that they are into the night made orgasmic until we become morning dew itself, bright and shining.

—Raymond Luczak
Minneapolis, Minnesota

Ebb stung by the flow, and flow stung by the ebb . . . . loveflesh swelling and deliciously aching,

Limitless limpid jets of love hot and enormous . . . . quivering jelly of love . . . whiteblow and delirious juice . . .

—Walt Whitman, *Leaves of Grass* (1855)

The dirtiest book in all the world is the expurgated book!

—Walt Whitman, 9 May 1888

Say Yes

after Walt Whitman (1819-1982)

Say yes.
Say yes to the breeze of a gentle dawn in a grassy field in
    June
and yes to the raging gale that whips November waves to
    frigid mountains.
Say yes to the north south east and west, to the winter
    spring and summer fall,
to the up and down and the he and him and you of youth.
Say yes to the iridescence of a dragonfly wing in the utter
    stillness of summer,
yes while the click of beetles and buzz of brazen bees, the
    tremulous trills of hidden birds
compose a symphony to the ineffable *it*.
And say yes to the concert hall and the dancer who desired
    only you,
to the museum and the bridge and the masters of air.
Say yes to a cloak of snow and ice in your new-grown
    beard
and yes to the sweat on his hard left shoulder after a good
    long day.
Say yes with your voice and tongue, with your knee and
    thigh.
Say it again and again from coast to coast and into the sea,
from border to border and beyond the borders,
yes to the believer and the unbeliever and the fluttering
    moment of decision
on the atom's edge of believing or unbelieving.
Say yes to the memory of the comrades fallen in futile
    wars,
withered by plague that left a mere lingering ghost of their
    rapt magnificence.
Say yes to your dreams and idle fantasies,

to the trivial and significant alike,
say yes to every color of skin or hair or eye.
Say yes to the sacred fire in the night, wrapped in your
    lover's arms or the arms of the never-ending yes.
Say yes as loud and as long as you can.
Say it and sing it, declare it, announce and sign it,
break awkward pauses with the resounding infinite word.

Say yes when your hair grows gray
and the arms that have held men grow frail and weary,
yes when the long sitting and frequent sleeping claim your
    daylight hours.
Say yes when, finally, it comes,
the great darkness or eternal light.
And whatever it is when it comes, let it hear you.
Let it hear you with your dying breath,
let it hear you say yes.
And as the memory of your greatest love kisses your
    eyelids one final time,
say yes.
Whisper or bellow it in your unwinding heart.
Say yes.

Athens Remembers

after Constantine Cavafy (1863-1933)

The ship from Alexandria to Athens had calm seas.
At the dock, a dark Adonis offered him a calloused hand
to step ashore. Once he made his own way in the world
but he was grateful for the handsome sailor's kindness.

At the old hotel, the desk clerk smiled, not in bold or
bashful invitation to a sun-bronzed man of muscle, but
a habitual gesture of welcome. Another lad, young
enough to be his son carried his bag to a small room.

Athens was on strike and the monuments were closed,
except the ones that weren't. At the old temple of the
Olympian Zeus, he recalled the nights when men and cats
prowled here. Now the columns seemed incongruous.

At the antiquities museum, alone among the army of
carved and cast relics of Hellenic glory, he lost himself
in a bust of Antinous, who drowned himself so his lover
would remember him always in the apogee of his youth.

His feet easily found the dark narrow street to the boy
brothel. He chose a tall, broad-shouldered *kouras* and
negotiated terms from a list of the usual options. It was
all as familiar as ordering a meal from a favorite café.

Upstairs, in dim light and music from a new world, they
joined in ancient ways he remembered vaguely. The
scent of young skin had faded. Gone was the tension
of deep breathing and breath held seemingly forever.

In the shower, they washed each other from their limbs.
The meager water was tepid, but the boy remained friendly

and soaped his back. Later in the hotel, he relived his hour with a boy named Kostas with mixed regret and
    satisfaction.

How to Write a Poem for Yves

after Assotto Saint (1957-1994)

You will be riding the Ninth Avenue bus toward home
when you pass again the white-brick building
where he lived with his Jaan, the compact apartment with the
tiny terrace. You sat laughing there with friends and sat
    weeping with his mother in the blink
of an eye.

Tell your mind to change the subject—quickly.
Listen to the living city all around you and
know that the time has come.

You will tell yourself to let it happen, no matter how
    reluctant you are to trace the loss again.
Let yourself fill with the memories of him, the open flower
    of him
and the dried flower, too, pressed into the Bible
of your heart.

Face the blank page as you would an Inquisitor.

How can you put it?
You embarked on an island cruise with a poet named Yves
and would up circumnavigating a globe you never knew
    existed.

To start, you will remember it was Carl who introduced
    you,
Carl who is dead now too,
the night you met so many others
you guard as fiercely as the Voodoo *gads* of his Haitian
    home.

Yves Lubin he was born and raised
and Assotto Saint he baptized himself in the blazing
    crucible
of his work and words:
Dancer, singer, actor, poet,
an incarnation of all nine muses set to music by
his Swedish Jaan.

You will try to remember the words he was reading when
you first laid eyes on him, tall, dark, mysterious, and
    magnificent,
his voice a ripe mango,
his eyes so innocently sadly wise
over the gleam of his sky-high cheeks and the
cryptic promise of his carnal lips
wrapping around vowels and nouns with erotic intentions.

Know he swam in seas of passion you will never know,
however long you sail, crossed continents of courage
and scaled mountain after mountain without
looking back or down even as the noose of
the advancing plague tightened around us all.

When he tells you he carries the virus,
smile ever so slightly and nod your head knowingly.
Hear the roar of a wind tunnel in your inner ear.
Breathe. Just breathe.
This isn't the first time you've heard a death sentence
and it won't be the last.
Decide in that moment to tie your future to his,
this master of the astonishing who flew through moods
as fast as a swift and deeper than indigo.

He wrote. He raged. He acted up as friend after friend
fell to the incalculable cruelty of pneumonia and
    carcinoma.

Still he wrote, still he lifted his entire tribe,
gay black men on the vanguard of transformation.
Some told the truth as a last act of defiance as their
    muscles
wasted and they grew too weak to stand or sit or even
move at all.
Yves refused to let their voices die.

The death of his Jaan would be the turning point,
the crux and culmination of his frenzied animation.
He grieved as decline set in,
and he tried to finish his life before it was over.

Remember:
When the time came that he could no longer hold a pen,
it seems, he silently agreed
to take his leave.

Try to think of something to say to his mother as she rocks
beside her dying son, nurse at his birth,
nurse again so far north in so alien a world,
hovering while Yves slips in and out of sleep.

Ask how it was even possible:
The man whose smile was as wide an archipelago
was already gone and the paper hand you held
was nothing but a sketch of him.

Go to the wake.
Hold your lover's hand.
Sit on the side of the room where his friends are sitting.
Look at the faces of his family sitting opposite and
try to conjure intersecting circles in place of opposite poles.

Look at the shell of him displayed in his box, his last
    appearance
on any stage.

Think that this log of him floating in a stagnant pond is as
little like the soaring juniper of the man
as a sigh is to a symphony.

Write:
He was a rain forest,
and leave it at that.

Ask:
Do the rituals of death ease pain at all,
or do the codices of unanswered questions
explain even so small a thing as a fairyfly's wing?

In the end:
he was born;
he lived—in saturated colors;
he loved with limbs and language,
with purpose and fervor, but
fell into a vortex impossible to withstand.

And so he died, his one tossed sapling ripped up by the
    roots
in the force of a hurricane.

Wish you could put into words what the miracle of him
meant to you as he walked his patch of earth.
Wish you could make the loss less lasting, less immense.
Wish that the blazing cosmic light didn't kill the star,
this wounded dancer, this fallen Saint.

In the end you can think only of this
and pray it will suffice:

Once, in the darkest time of the world,
I met a man named Yves,
and that made all the difference.

In Frank's Day

after Frank O'Hara (1926-1966)

If I had been you,
I would have strolled up 6th Avenue
and bought cartons of French cigarettes,
bottles of Italian liqueur,
and an issue of *The New York Post*
before Rupert Murdoch owned it.
Even though I'd be sad that Billie Holiday died,
I'd be glad the Post reported it on the front page.
I'd head out to East Hampton,
and when I got off the train
it would be the East Hampton of that time.
There would be no McMansions,
only crumbling old mansions
and affordable cottages in the Springs.
I'd drink the Italian liqueur
and smoke the French cigarettes
all weekend long without giving a thought
to lung cancer or cirrhosis of the liver.
I'd bask in the sun without applying sunscreen.
I would never have heard of AIDS
and I wouldn't know this happiness would end in 1966
on Fire Island one month after my fortieth birthday
in a chance encounter with a dune buggy.

Dear Federico

after Federico García Lorca (1898-1936)

It's late. I've stood for hours
watching swallows strike
and swivel at the insects'
commas. The certain
circling they commit to
feed themselves. We first
acknowledged one another
on the bridge above their frenzy,
in the growing dark. We tethered
together, all pause and follow,
while streetlights burst
amber over tulip poplars
that guide the river's dark cord.

On the empty steps
of my apartment, you offer
me a cigarette and I take
it simply to touch your hand,
even though I haven't smoked
in years. Federico, I don't understand
your poems with their silver-
lipped volcanoes and your
obsession with the dangers
of the moon: all salted, all boot
crushed, all clovered in mold.

As if I dreamt the careful linen
of your shirt, the undoing of the black
slick of your hair in the concrete's shy
heat. I was afraid you'd mistake
my hesitation for the bleeding of juniper
into the air, the long tongue of the sky
refusing, a zipper's seam split open.

Faith

after W. H. Auden (1907-1973)

> Lay your sleeping head my love,
> human on my faithless arm
> —"Lullaby"

Asleep, his body driftless, it's easy
to imagine how he'd been—

unfaithful—is that what to call
the opposite of faithful, un- implying

he had to pour something off
to act, as though he'd been brimming

with it prior? It sounds as if
a Pentecostal preacher had blustered

onto the scene: "Do you want
to be full of faith? Say yes!"

the chorus wavering with the organ's
pedaled vibrato. I want to lean

into that yes, but every day
I look to the coworker endlessly talking

gym routine, who pushes up
his sleeves displaying faithfulness,

showy, overblown, but I gaze
at the locker room's proffered

fruit, as my love must too. If I resist
un- would -less correct? Faithless?

Not that I am less for looking, but
if I'd had no faith at all—our years

all jest—predestined to fail? We
humans so flawed that our love

must break us. Are you faithful?
How should I condemn the man

I love, though my anger convinces
me I don't, but I know I will love

again, his guilty and beautiful head.

Duplex

after Claude McKay (1889-1948)

Don't accuse me of sleeping with your man
When I didn't know you had a man.

> Back when I didn't know you had a man,
> The moon glowed above the city's blackout.

I walked home by moonlight through the blackout.
I was too young to be reasonable.

> He was so young, so unreasonable,
> He dipped weed in embalming fluid.

He'd dip our weed in embalming fluid.
We'd make love on trains and in dressing rooms.

> Love in the subway, love in mall restrooms.
> A bore at home, he transformed in the city.

What's yours at home is a wolf in my city.
You can't accuse me of sleeping with a man.

JERICHO BROWN

Of My Fury

after Gerard Manley Hopkins (1844-1889)

I love a man I know could die
And not by way of illness
And not by his own hand
But because of the color of that hand and all
His flawless skin. One joy in it is
Understanding he can hurt me
But won't. I thought by now I'd be unhappy
Unconscious next to the same lover
So many nights in a row. He readies
For bed right on the other side
Of my fury, but first, I make a braid of us.
I don't sleep until I get what I want.

After Essex Hemphill

(1957-1995)

The night is the night. So
Say the stars that light us
As we kneel before one
Another, illegal and illegal
Like Malcolm X. This is
His park, this part
Of the capital where we
Say please with our mouths
Full of each other, no one
Hungry as me against this
Tree. This tree, if we push
Too hard, will fall. But if
I don't push at all, call me
A sissy. Somebody ahead
Of me seeded the fruit-
Bearing forest. The night
Is my right. Shouldn't I
Eat? Shouldn't I repeat,
It was good, like God?

Token

after A. E. Housman (1859-1936)

Burg, boro, ville, and wood,
I hate those tiny towns,
Their obligations. If I needed
Anyone to look at me, I'd dye my hair purple
And live in Bemidji. Look at me. I want to dye
My hair purple and never notice
You notice. I want the scandal
In my bedroom but not in the mouths of convenience
Store customers off the nearest highway. Let me be
Another invisible,
Used and forgotten and left
To whatever narrow miseries I make for myself
Without anybody asking
What's wrong. Concern for my soul offends me, so
I live in the city, the very shape of it
Winding like the mazes of the adult video outlets
I roamed in my 20s: pay a token to walk through
Tunnels of men, quick and colorless there where we
Each knew what we were,
There where I wasn't the only one.

Two Nude Sailors, Spooning in Their Bunk-bed Aboard a Nuclear Submarine

after Walt Whitman (1819-1892)

"Indomitable, untamed as thee."
—from "Song for All Seas, All Ships"

Nothing to see. Somewhere undisclosed in the Pacific,
A propeller pushes—and tailplanes guide—the boat
Forward: Circle after   circle after circle, the
Seawater about them   whirled into whatever
Waits—some immortal *shhhhhhhhh*,   a face
Bordering on reverence, its full depth
Defined by the dark, with cold, tiny mouths drifting
About the trench (such   a fall, no light will ever
Reach the innermost crag.   Watch now,   onboard,
As one hand intertwines with the other's:
Eyes shut all this time,   providing a little proof
Of the vision unseen: each lid fluttering—.
Moving past the two men asleep, others, indifferent,
Continue to work in shifts—   until dawn
Blurs the waters above: those muddied purple bands
And bright ribbons   with gray, imminent rings.
Although such words may never turn out to be
That much comfort—   ultimately—please say
Them with me now: The world is small.
The world is small, and full of vast, invincible things.

Unexpectedly

after Paul Monette (1945-1995)

Like Patrick grabbing me by the hand
on that crowded, jostling subway car
so many years ago.

He dragged me out the door,
to the Between
to the space between the cars
as we crossed the Brooklyn Bridge—
well, Brooklyn Bridge or Manhattan or whatever bridge—
it didn't matter because
standing on the small lip of the cars I was caught
unexpectedly
by the crashing hummmmmmmmmm of traffic above, the
    the rattle of the wind in my ears,
and the starry headlights
and their kin reflected in the flickering/shattering/
    splintering face of the water
so far, far below,
and the taste of a huge city I could only comprehend as a
    painted backdrop on a movie set, and the empty lots,
    and the ruins of a burned building,
the old fire smoke still reeking of all the cigars ever
    smoked in those fallen down, charred stores,
and the building lights like stars, and the stars, and
    dark, and the crashingrollingtempo of the subway car
    cocooned in graffiti as we hurtled through the night.

There's got to be a poem tucked away somewhere in those
    ruins.

Glass and Smoke

after Tennessee Williams (1911-1983)

I crashed around Island Park, kicking up scuttling leaves,
    and muttered "... like bits of a shattered rainbow ..." over
    and over while dreaming of playing Tom. The closest
    I got was gluing the menagerie back together after
    curtain call. But still it was enough.

And now I feel the urge to pace outside, my head full of
    words shattering against each other in a way to describe
    you. Shattering to be reformed into new derivations,
    new meanings, new signs.

I'm so much older now than that young man hoping to
    inherit Tom. I can taste the memories of that want and
    the smoke I inhaled to blow on stage and create the
    Moon Lake Casino, just as I can recall the crunch of
    leaves and the cold autumn wind.

Oh, how I desired the love jets of your words to shoot
    through me.

Beggar's Velvet

> *"There is no need to do any housework at all.*
> *After the first four years the dirt doesn't get any worse."*
> —Quentin Crisp (1908-1999)

It's Rumpelstiltskin you're most like,
except for the straw,
and especially the girl.

What you used was the everyday accumulation of hair,
    skin flakes, and dust that gathered in sheets across
    mantelpieces,
also known as approbation and repulsion and violence,
the arson perpetuated on your stately homo being,
but the 4,000 year-old fae strength was your spindle used
    to create wit, charm, and elegance
and, of course, with a lavender tint.

The Answer to Dandelions

after Clayton L. Valli (1951-2003)

I first read the word "alien" in a comic book and mentally
   pronounced it wrong. I pronounced it "Alan."

In the 1930 census, on one of the brittle brown pages as
   fragrant as a tobacco leaf my long dead gramma's name
   is written and next to it was the word "alien."

Had something similar happened to my grandmother when
   she married a foreigner? Was she reduced to *de sotto
   voce*, hidden behind hands?

Among Deaf people I've seen unpleasant topics disappear
   from their normal signing chest space down to their
   waists.

Clayton, our hands are dandelion roots ripped out and left
   to wilt for the world to ignore. We can't let each other
   disappear.

Bite Hard

for Justin Chin (1969-2015)

Would've made it
to his deathbed had I

not been pulled over—

the backseat filled
with Get-Well balloons

and as it happens

I was in white face
wearing a red rubber

nose, knowing

that would've made
my friend on life support

laugh—the neighbor

next door who happened
to hear a loud crash

instinctively calling

911 till someone
kicked my friend's

door in—the whole

palliative shit show
coming to an end

when they yanked

the plug before
I had the chance to

get there and wouldn't

you know the cop
who pulled me over

was black, was taken

slightly aback
at my clowning around,

wondering if he was

waking up in a bad
dream as I reassured him

no, this is America,

not some third-world
ass-fucked place where

law and order no

longer rule, go ahead
and administer

your Breathalyzer,

allow me to prove
to you I'm still

alive underneath

this mask, and yes,
as a model minority

I do sucky fucky

for five dolla' so long
as you're willing to

keep it zipped—

Meet Me Under the Whale

for Reginald Shepherd (1963-2008)

I don't remember what hour we
met, only that the room

was hot. I don't remember

if there was even a clock
presiding, only that someone

had stolen the hands

off its face, eyes already
darting under the table—slips

of tongue like paper cuts

we would get to suck on
while a chanteuse nonchalantly

took the stage. You looked

at me like a worm crawling
on a glass globe, waiting

for something to come along

and pluck you off. Seems
like we'd been ordering

off the same menus for years

only the prices had changed—
note for note, the songs

no longer recognizable

as we rode into the mouth
of a whale full of untold

myths, staircases spiraling

down. It hardly matters now
who asked for the check

or even who paid, how much

everyone got tipped. We
were in there for a long time

trying to decide—Master

the Tempest is Raging
tinged with its laissez-faire

jazz while our lady leaned on

a baby grand, her combs
inlaid with mother of pearl

thrown down—bleached bones

and tongues of the damned
washing up on shore

in the corners of our eyes.

Ars Poetica

for J. D. McClatchy (1945-2018)

Careful what you write

on the title
page of a book

someone wants you

to inscribe. Could easily
find its way

to those dusty shelves

of a used
bookstore both of you

will happen to

patronize decades from now
when whatever good

feeling that still exists

between you will
have used itself up

for it really can't

be helped you know
all those words

you've managed to leave

behind as testament
to things you thought

would last but

didn't. The question now
remains: do you

buy back the thing

at a deep
discount, hold out for

the right moment

to give that someone
a second chance

by re-gifting the thing

in some shiny
paper even your mother

would find hard

to resist? Or do
you stand there

way in the back

of the store
where the cashier is

not likely to

see you rip out
what you inscribed

though the price

of the book suggests
your signature

has increased the value

of something someone
didn't really want

only now that too

seems for naught
for whoever is dumb

enough to pay

for it will find
themselves taking home

such a tiny act

of vanity from which
no one

seems to be immune—

Once I Start Remembering So Much Comes Back
after Tim Dlugos (1950-1990)

> "It's strange how quickly / hospitals feel
> foreign / when you leave, and how normal
> / their conventions seem as soon / as you
> check in."
>
> —"G-9"

Sometime I forget I was alive
when men were making their lists of the dead—
of the sick—of the dying—in New York—
in San Francisco—in LA.
Cities I've been to.
Cities I've survived.
But I was alive.
A boy in Indiana
and then a teenager
seeing news of a plague
and then those made-for-TV movies
and then later the lectures on condoms
and then maybe even the hint of fear
in my mother's face
when I finally told her I was gay.
Even though she knew better.
We all did by then.
And how I ended up here
in New York
where every spot marks a death
where older men show me
their battle wounds
where myths take hold
rearrange the story.
Defense mechanisms in full effect.
Where I now work alongside men
and women who were there.

Who saw more death than any human ever should.
Who survived.
And now I go out each night
into the dark
into sex clubs—the ones that still exist.
Down the stairs
where the blacklight greets me
where my teeth shine
as I smile at the doorman—the sex party host.
How I talk to men about fucking.
How I test them.
Give them results
that don't mean what they once meant
and how I talk about a pill
that can stop infection.
How some men tell me of anxiety
built into their bodies
how they can't shake the fear
how scars don't leave us
even after they heal.
My body moves so easily
in these spaces
then back to the clinic
where language is in code:
abbreviations for everything.
Why can no one use full words?
I'm a poet floating in the medicine.
Drowning in the letters.
The dark spaces
are where I feel most at home
where sounds of fucking
are my work rhythm
like the beating drum of life
that hasn't given up—hasn't stopped.
Not yet.
Never will.

And how I go home at night
and reread "G-9"—how it can still make me cry
and I don't even know
if he would want that: these tears.
And I wonder what I would say
if anyone ever asked me
what were the best years of my life—
of my life in New York—
could I say "Today"?
What about tomorrow?

Comrade

after Walt Whitman (1819-1892)

Lie down in the trenches with me,
Comrade,
in our field of war
where we survive together
and hope not to survive the other.
We will listen for shells
and nurse each other's wounds
when hit. We will
keep up morale
by telling stories about
our lives before.
I will worry when you scout ahead
and miss you until you return.
We will do what we can
to lift each other up
and never keep
the other down.
And we will lie together,
in the trenches,
and it will be our war,
and we will never hope for peace.

Love Poetry and the Reader

Upon rereading Constantine Cavafy (1863-1933)

how strange—now everything is gone, the fleshy lips and
thick chest from the shadows a century ago, as well as
the thirst-ravaged mind that gazed longingly upon them—
still, it is strange—the strings of words which furtively
recorded those things continue to live and breathe,
still send me, the reader, into overheated bewilderment—
but stranger yet—not so long from now, I too
will vanish completely, leaving not a trace behind

(Translated by Jeffrey Angles)

With Twig in Hand

*On the forty-eighth anniversary of
the death of Shinobu Orikuchi (1877-1953)*

The ghosts which came, accompanied by the mosquitoes'
buzz,
Invited by burning hemp and softly sobbing flute, now
retreat
Each of us carries a machilus twig in hand
To this sandy graveyard along the wind-swept shore
One spirit—beloved, young, also a son—
The other—loving, older, a father—in a double grave
In the sand before it, we stick our twigs, place them
perhaps
Foreheads bent, we clap our hands in prayer, then disband
In fact, this gravestone is for all of us here in the world
The two spirits will dissolve into the sky over time and
As we leave here, our steps will carry us to the celestial
shore,
Each of us carrying an invisible twig in our hands

(Translated by Jeffrey Angles)

Don't Remember, Can't Forget

after Joe Brainard (1942-1994)

I don't remember the scalpel or the ether.

I can't forget the scar.

I don't remember the Silly Putty or the orange chair
cushion.

I can't forget the scar.

I don't remember the missing red stuffed-animal monkey
with the hard, rubber face.

I can't forget the scar.

I don't remember the jokes about having blonde hair and
the milkman.

I can't forget the scar.

I don't remember the picnic table, the sudden bruising grab,
the shame.

I can't forget the scar.

I don't remember the handsome soldier who made my aunt
cry.

I can't forget the scar.

I don't remember sleepwalking, peeing in a bowl of my
parents' popcorn.

I can't forget the scar.

I don't remember the yellowing, cracking clear plastic
covering the white sofa.

I can't forget the scar.

I don't remember when the younger brother began to
overpower the older one.

I can't forget the scar.

I don't remember shoplifting Lik-M-Aid, watermelon Jolly
Ranchers and Butterfinger.

I can't forget the scar.

I don't remember the first boy to call me faggot.

I can't forget the scar.

I don't remember the first time Billy kissed me.

I can't forget the scar.
I don't remember forgetting the lines of dialogue, the
     words to the song in the play.
I can't forget the scar.
I don't remember gazing at *The Barbra Streisand Album*
     cover, making my mouth the same shape.
I can't forget the scar.
I don't remember kissing Paul McCartney and John
     Lennon's pictures on *Meet the Beatles*.
I can't forget the scar.
I don't remember playing with my sister's Barbie dolls,
     whether she was there or not.
I can't forget the scar.
I don't remember Poco pulling too hard on her leash, the
     icy sidewalk, the broken finger.
I can't forget the scar.
I don't remember my traveling salesman father's heavy
     sample cases, the long road trips.
I can't forget the scar.
I don't remember my mother being unable to leave the
     house for days at a time.
I can't forget the scar.
I don't remember having sex with Aaron in my brother's
     lower bunk.
I can't forget the scar.
I don't remember the Duster's leaky gas tank and the fire
     engines.
I can't forget the scar.
I don't remember crying on the Amtrak train at Union
     Station before leaving for Boston.
I can't forget the scar.
I don't remember the electric sensation of having my first
     poem published in a magazine.
I can't forget the scar.
I don't remember the lovers' quarrels and the make-up sex
     with John on Prince Street.

I can't forget the scar.
I don't remember the first time I read about the "rare
cancer seen in 41 homosexuals."
I can't forget the scar.
I don't remember saying goodbye to Rolando in the AIDS
ward at St. Joseph's Hospital.
I can't forget the scar.

Sebastian at Siege

for Marcel Proust (1871-1922)

Mother, the air is a thief.
It steals salt from the body, loosens
the Will, until it splays out, liquid.
I sit straight up in bed, naked,
looking in the mirror. This, my body,
which I consume. The tendons
and frets on which it hangs.
Hating it once, it is now so beautiful, dying
in its time. Learning how to learn, to whistle
with the starlings, names a tender absolution.
In this Byzantine chamber, the air
makes a fist. An angel
bursting through the chalice of the flesh.
In these catacombs I perfect my sweat.

A Welcome to the Black Sun

for James Baldwin (1924-1987)

Be patient. How
can I be patient?

From your lips I sip
clear water, drops

clinging to mine.
From the branches,

your arms,
turtledoves.

From your skin
indigo seeps,

spreading over mine.
But from your being

proud lions roar
across the grasses

of my days. The fields'
camphor lights

ignite mine.
Mercy! Mercy!

the goldenrod cries.
and small rabbits

run through the grass.
Be patient. How?

When wheat
kernels pop even now

in the solitary heat?
and your lips draw a necklace

of rain down my cheeks,
mingling clean water

with scalding kisses?

Physical Love

for Jean Genet (1910-1986)

Can one measure
the circumference? Or can
one by palm and fingers
estimate the length?
Is it the darkness at the base,
the curls, the flicker in
the shadows, which most attracts?
Or is it
density?
Who can name its sweetness?

Probing the resistance, how can I
reach the tower, then
defect, slipping down
abruptly to the bottom,
glancing
in the shuttle brilliancy
of hair? It is
a throat
of melancholy compressed to
a purple wrinkle. A polleniferous
sack of
sensation, and rose.
To pass one's hand among the leaves,
harsh on the upper surface, soft
beneath.
The faint, dusk scent.
The fruit's neck yellows
as it joins the branch.
Then.
Handling the fruit.
Honey
moisture dripping at the eye.

One blooms gray with it—
the low-toned blush
from purple
to pink.
Oh joy!
The luscious pulp
so much afraid and so
courageous.
and madly, you take
the rise,
the boldness,
leaning, looking
down,
and elated, stricken
with terror, the sun-
light drives through your
dark caverns.

JEFFERY BEAM

That Night

for Walt Whitman (1819-1892)

That body	tree on a misty hill
That face	fawn with dark eyes
That full moon	surrounded by evening skies
That hour	pavement ending in dust
That grass	green with summer's black-green
That night	coming over us with its breath
That sound	crickets singing at eye level
That body	me on the ground with their song
That body	another touching me with fire
That fire	round as the moon burning as the sun
That face	fawn with dark eyes
That you	speaking in tongues unknown and green
That sound	crickets singing in my ear
That body	tree on a misty hill

ALEX GILDZEN

Body Parts

after Walt Whitman (1819-1892)

"from top to toe I sing"
—Walt Whitman

GUY MADISON'S HAIR

a forest
for fingers
to linger
in

JOHNNY DEPP'S EYES

turn coal
into gems

OWEN WILSON'S NOSE

let me slip
down it
then climb
back up

again

CALVIN LOCKHART'S EARS

my tongue
never tires
in there

ALEX GILDZEN

JUDE LAW'S LIPS

this map
to ecstasy
makes
travelers
of us
all

RUPERT EVERETT'S CHIN

the hillock
that anchors
his face
harbors lust
that zooms
from him
to me

LESLIE CHEUNG'S NECK

long
slow
glide

to ah

ALDO RAY'S CHEST

have you ever
playd in a garden
& never wantd
to leave?

JOEL McCREA'S ARMPITS

whether hirsute
or not
his suit
me fine

JEFF BRIDGES'S BACK

latissimus dorsi in carrara:
to look at

but to feel:
warm apple pie trapezius

JOHN BROMFIELD'S NAVEL

an urn
which earns
my sweat

SAL MINEO'S PUBIS

such ache
that arch
causd

my body
knew
before
I did

ALEX GILDZEN

GAEL GARCIA BERNAL'S ASS

I'm an astronaut
planting a flag
                    there

ALEXIS ARQUETTE'S COCK

wait
        while I
invent
        a new language

BRAD PITT'S THIGHS

I cd spread
a picnic there

feast of juice
& tender meat

I cd lick
the flesh there

then wipe lips
knowing I will

remember his name

GEORGE NADER'S KNEES

islands
            on an oblong map

that snaps open
                    when
I dream
of boyhood

TAB HUNTER'S LEGS

another list:
all the tasks
I ask
them to tackle

RICHARD HARRISON'S ANKLES

o
the
vowels
they
offer

HUGH DANCY'S TOES

make me
want to dance

ALEX GILDZEN

Alone in Cleveland

after Hart Crane (1899-1932)

no Wasco so
dinner plans dumpd

I walk from hotel
to Greek Isles to find it
no longer there

on way back
I cut thru the Arcade
under its glass arch
time becomes a jumble

can it be 40 years
since I bought my first book
from Jim Lowell here?

I sit at end of stairs
around corner from that
other famous bookshop
the one Hart Crane hauntd

I look up at gilt balconies
& there he is

he's alone in Cleveland
I'm alone in Cleveland

I wink at him & he smiles
we meet at the Euclid entrance

"permit me to be
yr sailor for the nite"

he looks nervously both ways
then takes my hand
& kisses it

next morning
on way to airport
I glance at the spot
touchd by his lips

I see a word

now every nite I'm alone
I see that word
& the lips that left it
I see Hart Crane in the Arcade
smiling at me

& that word jumps
to paper
& I'm not alone
anymore

What I Remember about Chris

after Joe Brainard (1942-1994)

I remember the night we met. It was at X-mart, this store
   that sold adult toys and videos. There was a sex arcade
   with booths in the back where people could watch porn.

I remember thinking that you were homeless walking in
   back with a very thick beard and cap pulled low on your
   head.

I remember how sore my jaw was after sucking your dick
   in one of the booths.

I remember us exchanging phone numbers in the parking
   lot.

I remember not wanting to call you out of being afraid that
   you would want a repeat performance, and thinking
   that my jaw most likely would not hold out, but I called
   you anyway.

I remember your dick growing to be very hard.

I remember your silver PT Cruiser.

I remember writing you love letters.

I remember writing poems about you.

I remember telling you that I was in love with you.

I remember there was a time when you were all that I
   thought about.

I remember sitting outside of your apartment building in
   hopes that I would catch a glimpse of you.

I remember sneaking to the back of your apartment and
   peeking in through the sliding glass to watch you sleep.

I remember buying you DVDs, clothes and giving you
   money.

I remember seriously thinking about getting Property of
   Chris tattooed on my arm, or my ass.

I remember a Monday afternoon blow job.

I remember giving you a blow job in my dad's truck.

I remember your black leather sofas.

I remember your apartment on Chapel Drive never ever being clean.

I remember that Dalmatian you had.

I remember when you worked as a manager at Seminole Bowl.

I remember bringing you lunch to work.

I remember sitting in the parking lot waiting to pick you up.

I remember how handsome you looked in a gray suit.

I remember thinking that I would do anything for you.

I remember wanting to kiss you.

I remember giving you a blow job as you drove my car back to your parent's house from Wal-Mart. When I tried to sit up out of your lap, you said, "No, stay down, someone is coming."

I remember the hair on your back that grew in patches.

I remember you telling me that you didn't like soul food.

I remember putting way too much oil on popcorn that day we went to the movies.

I remember you telling me that you wished we had become friends first before ever doing anything sexual.

I remember when we went joyriding while we got drunk off Crown Royal.

I remember us eating hot wings and drinking beer at BW3's.

I remember how annoyed I would get when you would strike up a conversation with a complete stranger in the bar about baseball or basketball.

I remember giving you car head in your parent's driveway.

I remember your large collection of porn.

I remember blowing you in your parent's living room. You stripped naked and slipped one of the porn DVDs I brought.

I remember when the girlfriend called. I thought how ballsy you were for talking to her as I blew you.

I remember not being very interested when you went on and on about your oral sex skills on women.

I remember asking you who gave the best blow jobs, me or the girlfriend.

I remember sending you several text messages a day.

I remember calling and always getting your voicemail.

I remember after every argument we had, saying that I would never talk to you again, yet I never stuck to that.

I remember in instance where I cried on the phone when you told me that you didn't want to talk to me anymore because the girlfriend was getting jealous and angry.

I remember you referring to semen as "nut."

I remember jacking off as I thought of your dick.

I remember swallowing your *nut*.

I remember when you told me you won ninety dollars playing scratch offs.

I remember leaving a note on the windshield of your car.

I remember giving you a copy of a story I wrote about you. When you told me that your girlfriend found it, you blamed me.

I remember getting a phone call from a bails bondsman telling me that you were in jail and you wanted to see me.

I remember how the lobby of the jail smelled faintly of bleach and feet.

I remember going to visit you every day until you told me that I didn't need to come every day.

I remember that awful blue and white uniform you had to wear and the white plastic sandals.

I remember wanting to give you everything.

I remember feeling that you were using me, but I didn't much care.

I remember wondering for so long what the girlfriend looked like and when I found out, I couldn't understand what you saw in her.

I remember you living out of a motel. You refused to pay rent because the landlord said he wouldn't replace the carpet after a toilet pipe burst.

I remember fly paper that hung from the ceiling of your bedroom.

I remember the girlfriend refusing to visit you when you were locked up.

I remember thinking how brave you were for deciding to do jail time instead of being on probation.

I remember how angry I was that night I saw those two girls follow you into your apartment one late Friday night. You later told me that one of them blew you while the other one ended up passing out.

I remember you telling me to calm down.

I remember wondering why you never called the cops once you figured out that I was stalking you.

I remember getting French Silk chocolate ice cream on my shirt after we went out for ice cream.

I remember how warm your hips felt.

I remember how hairy your ass felt.

I remember you telling me that you were in high school when you began messing around with guys.

I remember you telling me that you were more attracted to Kelly Rowland over Beyoncé.

I remember being quite desperate to have sex with you. You were always coming up with excuses.

I remember realizing that you were a complete sociopath.

I remember sometimes being repulsed by you.

I remember your girlfriend texting me pretending to be you.

I remember the only time we could hang out was when the girlfriend was out of town.

I remember seeing your dad and thinking that you look exactly like him.

I remember wondering if your dad was just as well-endowed as you.

I remember your dad being a total DILF.

I remember after years of being in love with you and obsessing, I had finally snapped out of it.

This is Where Frank O'Hara Lives

(1926-1966)

Walk past Metro Drugs
where the items are drastically reduced.
The place of big savings, special offers.
Break past the well-dressed old ladies,
A woman with her baby wrapped in her arms.
Veer off the sidewalk, past a parking meter
To avoid running into a herd of hot guys.
One of them is wearing the shoes I want.
Move past a woman digging for change
to save her Dodge Shadow from getting towed.
So excited. Going as fast as my Reeboks will take me.
Almost stepped in dog shit.
Almost kicked over a coffee cup
Of change belonging to some homeless guy.
Walk past Gotham Bar & Grill,
The bored employee in the box office of Cinema Village.
A few more steps. I'm getting warmer.
Can smell the ground beef from Big Enchilada.
There goes 12th Street Books.
Better slow down, don't want to miss it.
There's the tiger-print lined journal I've been looking for.
Today's special is Mixed Bean Soup and Fresh Fried Squid.
Frank's place should be right around this corner.
Here it is.
He's sandwiched between a restaurant
That serves the best Japanese noodles;
A place that sells Cuisinart kitchen appliances.
That must be the window he sits in composing verse.
 He's got a great view of a Fed-Ex truck.
I'm leaning against a Civic E-X, its tinted windows,
I'm dying to meet him.
He's probably busy doing laundry or watching his favorite
    soap.

I wish he could come out and play.
We could sit in Union Square and watch all the cute guys
Walk by while we eat hot knish and drink cold sodas.

ARTHUR DURKEE

Walt Whitman's Summer Wander Across America
(1819-1892)

Walt Whitman arises from his warm bed in the cool just before dawn, before the day's heat waxes. He sets forth from his front door, after his morning ablutions, to walk boldly forth across the face of America. He strides out beyond the end of his door-path, past the end of the lane, and on outward into the wider world. His strides lengthen until his feet embrace cities, continents, worlds, the whole cosmic song of living. His lungs fill with crisp morning air. His eyes brim over with tree-shadows, the splendid laughter of young calves, the shining sun reflecting off mica chips along the trailside.

Walt Whitman is dazzled by the beauty of this world of flesh and radiance. He sets out on the open road from his city home in New York, and spreads his gaze across many roads West and North and South from his Long Island and New Jersey residences. He sets out along long roads every summer in search of the beauty of men revealed in play, in hope, in forgetfulness of winter and inwardness, as each summer the world is made bright anew. He strides forth into the world, his entire being filled with joy. He knows that joy will find a way, that ecstasy will get a hold on him, that no darkness can ever be depthless when kicked open to bleed sunlight. Every breath he takes as he walks ever greater into the world becomes the breath of life itself.

Walt Whitman is watching young men as they play a sandlot baseball game in windy green-hilled Iowa in early summer. Walt Whitman is silently watching the game, his eye following every catch, lusting in his heart after long clean limbs exposed to open air, the winged shoulders, strong wrists and thighs of the players, their bent backs and arcing shoulders as they throw or pause in running between the bases. He is sitting in the top row of bleachers at Wrigley Field, at Shea Stadium, his eyebrows leaping in good humor as crowds surge and dance with every action of the players on the field.

Walt Whitman is standing unobserved behind the chain-link fence around a basketball court in Oklahoma City. It's a sunny humid summer afternoon and the boys have taken off their shirts as they dance with the ball, shoulders and flanks and thighs and breasts and white-socked ankles slick with their own sweat, a sheen of mist on the body catching the gold-amber light of the setting sun.

Walt Whitman sets out on the open road late each spring and wanders all summer, watching the men and boys play their summer games. He spends hours in silver waterfalls that feed the Finger Lakes. He sits under a shade umbrella at poolside in every suburban metro swimming pool in the Great Plains states, where young men and old men and their sisters and mothers reveal their near-nudity to sun and endless wind, and frolic in clean clear blue chlorinated waters while the lifeguard in his red skimpy shorts watches over all with his whistle and gaze, his sunburned nose smeared with white zinc oxide cream.

Walk Whitman wanders down the street in a small town in Idaho where skater boys jump their boards again and again on the concrete and steel of public library steps till some authority figure chases them away, to return again after an hour's pause for sodas and rest. He sits on a boulder at the south fork of the American River near Auburn California where all the swimmers, men and women, remove their clothing to frolic nude in whitewater deep swimming holes, in pools of root-beer foam below the falls. He watches the swimmers play unselfconciously under cliffs and boulders, emerging with wet foreheads that shine radiantly in noon sun. He watches bathers lie back to sun themselves dry on the flat sheets of stone.

Walt Whitman contemplates the naked torsos of men and women he sees all across North America, revealed to summer sun, in heat haze or blaze of light, and loves them equally as beautiful expressions of physical grace that lasts only a few brief summers before growing stolid or flabby. He marvels at the perfect form of the human collarbone, the heart beating beneath, ribs expanding with short deep athletic breath. He sees the naked muscles and long limbs of bathers and athletes and sees in their revelation of their flesh a godlike animal beauty made more sensual still when flung into wild motion. Walt Whitman seeks a revelation of the sunbright beauty of the godbody-self in every place he visits along his saunter.

He finds revelation in western slot canyons where only the most adventurous hike, to finally strip off sweat-soaked shirts and dive into clear still pools of rainwater that rushes down from mountain steppes. He finds it in shallow rivers, banked and hidden behind groves of birch and maple, where someone has hung a rope tire swing over a blackwater swimming hole just upstream of a small Wisconsin farm town. He finds it at Coney Island, where the beach is covered with swarms of city people escaping urban smog on a Sunday afternoon, with ice cream stands and carnival rides and puffy white clouds overhead. He finds it south of San Francisco, at a gay nude beach between two coastal state parks, sheltered by cliffs and open to the Pacific Ocean, with tunneled caves in rock formations at the beach's north end where men steal together for hidden trysts as surf washes their ankles and thighs.

He finds it at a placid beach inside Florida's Gulf Coast, on a grey day under a grey sky before hurricane season has reached its peak, with a stiff wind raising goosebumps on the arms and breasts of boys and girls playing together making sand castles. He finds it under spreading ferns along the Appalachian Trail. He finds it where the white-flanked magpies soar over the Rio Grande canyon in New Mexico, the whitewater rafters have pulled into shore, beaching their Kevlar inflatables to serve the midday meal, suddenly in the heat everyone has stripped off their clothes to dive into cold fresh waters, their shouts echoing back and forth from canyon walls. He finds it at a hidden geothermal spring in Wyoming, in Oregon, in Montana, where the scalding waters rise to make a pool hidden down a dirt road a few miles off the state two-lane highway stitching itself across the long arid highland plateaus.

He finds it at an isolated mountain stream at Granite Pass in the Bighorn Mountains, at the Temperance River above Lake Superior in Minnesota, around the curve of sheltered trout waters near the headlands of the Hudson River in the Adirondacks. He finds it wherever overheated outdoor summer hikers and trout fisherman stop for a moment to bathe nude in refreshing cool waters. He finds it where the young men race their bicycles in Illinois. He finds it at the top of a gold sandstone cliff overlooking a highway hundreds of feet below at the apex of a long slickrock trail in Utah, in Arizona, in Texas.

He finds it on a flooded state park trail in southern Indiana after heavy rains have spilled the river over its banks, where young men take off their clothes to wade in the hot dappled shade and catch with bare hands trout swimming around the bases of trees. He finds it along the desert Rio Grande where owls watch nude swimmers cross at midnight, arriving as pilgrims to Gold Mountain to begin the long dry walk toward a dream of freedom. He finds it under an overhang of shelfrock in Tennessee where a small stream waterfall cascades into the deep gorge and undercuts the cliff just far enough for two to sit together and hold hands. He finds it on a 100 degree day in Brooklyn when the city opens up a fire hydrant so neighborhood kids can soak themselves and play in cool high-pressure city water for half an hour.

He finds it at the foot of a sinuous Henry Moore bronze in downtown Columbus Indiana, where tourists run with their children between guidebook attractions and views while young businessmen loosen ties and sit crosslegged to eat their lunches. He finds it where a group of rain-wet boys playing in Tucumcari New Mexico stop to admire a double rainbow appearing in the eastern skies. He finds it on a sticky afternoon in rural Alabama where a group of skinhead white boys take off their Doc Martens and ripped jeans to lie in a row on dirty sheets and masturbate together in a bedroom whose walls are draped with Confederate flags. He finds it in an isolated park in northern Michigan where people re-enact a fur-trade era rendezvous camp on a summer evening so humid that most of the men and boys have been wearing just loincloths all day and no one bothers getting dressed for dinner.

He finds it under the shelter of a shade tree hanging over the Brandywine River in Pennsylvania, where a group of college students have drifted out of the sun after rafting all morning in oversize truck inner tubes. The day has stilled, the air completely calm, everywhere is silence in which tufts of cottonwood seed float through the air, and a humming cicada call only deepens the silence. After a long nap, the young men wake at the same moment, and with no words passing between them, look into each other's eyes and as if with one will strip off their remaining clothes and float nude into the river current, only to fall back in couples under shade trees stretched far over the river bank, and bump together kissing. Walt Whitman knows how summer heat rises through long-limbed flesh and roots in the loins, making hearts race and eyes widen as the Great God Pan wanders like a wind-devil tornado through dusty streets, over riverbanks, in empty city lots, among wild mustangs of the wide basins between tall ranges. Walt Whitman knows that at any moment a langorous afternoon nap might waken into erotic self-pleasure, and afterwards sink back into a deeper sea of sleep.

Walt Whitman watches young men dancing together everywhere, strutting long legs in competitive display at a Greek wedding in Boston, bouncing the feathers and trains of their fancy dance costumes at a night powwow in Idaho, breathing intimately close together in a gay club in Florida where life-affirming music endlessly pulses, at a smoky discotheque in East L.A.

Walt Whitman sighs as stocky Navajo men refuse to come in out of the seasonal monsoon rain, instead getting drenched with faces raised into the storm, water streaming down their faces and making their shirts transparent. He watches dark-skinned and coffee-skinned boys sit on neighborhood stoops in Chicago and Albuquerque and Detroit, just hanging out doing nothing in sweltering evening gloom, their mocking laughter ringing out echoes off apartment windows across the street. Walt Whitman knows that the future belongs to all the brown and tan and chocolate and ebony peoples of the world, and is glad. He watches Indian and Latino boys play shirts-and-skins stickball in dusty driveways at the edges of their worlds between pueblo and city ways. He sees beautiful boys with long shiny black hair on the Pine Ridge reservation in South Dakota hiding in the prairie grass and wind-etched gullies playing cowboys-and-Indians, only the game keeps falling apart because everybody wants to play the winning Indians and nobody wants to play the loser cowboys.

Walt Whitman stands unobserved watching the erotic play of the tall prairie grass and sunflowers against the red sky of South Dakota evenings. He invisibly caresses the hair of joggers in Central Park. His spirit rests silently on the Indian burial mounds of southern Ohio. He walks between the tall pines never logged in central Michigan and contemplates the upraised prayer faces of shaded trillium. He smiles upon Lake Erie as it returns to unpolluted life brimful with perch and returning salmon. He leans against a basalt hexagon above Yellowstone Falls and watches eagles cavort and play.

Walt Whitman sighs near the end of summer afternoon, and opens his arms to wrestle with dandelions. He eloquently says nothing to ditch-lilies emerging orange near the railroad tracks. He shakes his head and smiles at the play of water-sprinklers on the unnatural lawns of retirement Arizona. He strolls unseen along streets and alleys in Minneapolis. His beard is full of sparrows and hummingbird moths. His mouth caresses the taste of lichen slowly digesting granite outcrops. He lays on his back amongst wildflowers and makes love to the whole sky.

Walt Whitman wanders along late summer blue highways till at last he stops to watch a pickup game in the last light of summer's end, in the heat of the night, where purple dusk picks out the last reflected sheen of stars on wet skin, till heaven looks down on the poet at last at peace, his breast full of visions memories and cherished locker-room smells.

Walt Whitman sleeps through the winter and rises again, a god of summer, to watch again the young men play through their lives in the heat and lingering sunlight and sweat of long summer evenings. He dreams, once again in his warm bed, of the dear love of comrades sleeping on river beaches arm-in-arm, breathing in unity as they lie side-by-side between crisp cotton sheets, stirring in their sleep to intertwine arms and legs and spoon in serene fulfillment without waking. In the Dreaming that is his memory of the beauty of love and skin and muscle sliding in the light, he reawakens and recreates and remakes the world. He sings the world into dancing being, the Poet who will come again to summer all over the land.

STUART BARNES

Happiness: A Cento

after Martin Harrison (1949–2014)

transformation happening as if marble turns to flesh
everything you give off moving faster than purest desert
    light
taking on a bluer tinge, a sculpted shape
and you infolding the world like it's a shape more familiar
    than air
opening up exactly what's required
making a mountain out of gravity's falling tissue
reorganising   how the heat takes over
gliding over stone and the shadows of those passing
the hillsides like a breath
drumming its fists on the verandah roof
and certainly patching up those palm-tree tops with far-off
    cumulus

        ·

carrying the thought of you, the touch of you,
body held explored crotch and cock
how you look at me   how you look back

        ·

outside the window
honey-eaters, blue wrens,
bouquets of white cockatoos bursting from the leaves
their speed so fine they look like dark flames

        ·

A drover playing his harmonica
to the flesh's range,
immense like Australian sky

.

words turning out later to be the simplest thoughts:
when I was born
like a ghost or a short, quick river
into country without water apart from winter rain
shaping and reshaping sideways through winter sun's
    white light—
recalled just now—
a neighbour—what are they doing out there?—dropping a
    trailer or a drum

.

knowing the world's renewable despite each paid-off
    politician.
on a backdrop of night,
they know nothing of life's burning colour.

.

suddenness which takes my breath away
(the slow dissolve, daybreak light on clouds like broccoli
    leaves)
the poem for you
meeting the air
The last view of the sea

.

We farmed it like we were angels.

At the End, a Virgin

after Constantine Cavafy (1863-1933)

You will come back someday, lost medal, lost bead, lost
   petal.
You will come back to me at the end and throw the
   numbers out, give them back their names, crown my
   graying curls with white flowers, crown my bald head
   with moss and clover.
You will come back and wash my face with a clean cloth.
   You will come back and show me that the cloth stays
   clean after you wash me.
You will come back and make me flower, make my mud
   flower, make my soil green, make my spring the kind of
   season that will invite sighs and myths and embroidery.
You will come back and make my fading fair, my fire fine,
   my ice clear enough to see the faces I entombed in it
   these years. You will come back and free the faces. You
   will come back and return them to their owners.
You will come back and tell me that want and need are
   equally guiltless, equally unnecessary. You will come
   back and tell me that the distinction between necessary
   and unnecessary isn't relevant. You will come back and
   make me believe it. You will come back and make me
   sigh and smile.
You will come back and give me a sieve to hold my regrets.
   We will sift them out together.
You will come back at the end and welcome me into the
   company into which I was born.

Careful Is Not An Art

for Tim Dlugos (1950-1990)

The sauna door opened from time to time; the steam
     thicker than the press of men,
(the "semeny love of comrades" you said), grunting in their
     abandon.
Alone in the wet heat, just watching, not touching,

          I couldn't see you, clouded,
          but heard you say,
"Why are you just standing around posing, honey?"

As you came closer, I laughed with embarrassment.
After a few caresses, elbows knocking, (but nothing much
     else), you told me your name.
          "Oh! I know your poetry!" and so we began to
     talk,
amid the hothouse whispers, of your books
and you mentioned so many poets I did not know.

Michael, Donald, James.

We chatted and chatted among all that sex going on,
and us the two lone voices, singing some song of ourselves.

          Someone shouted, "Suck, fuck, or leave!"

Towels saronged midriff, we continued the conversation
on cheap sofas beside the plastic flowers, near the weepy
     fountain and the
water-stained posters of well-hung men.

Amid the lessening footsteps of men who had gained or
     lost,

I began to fall asleep (we only had lockers that night).
At 4 a.m. we dragged ourselves out, both back home—by
     coincidence neighbors!—
to Brooklyn Heights.

Tim, I remember reading your "Catholic poems," and
drinking your gin, and the time you took me to hear you
     lecture
at Cooper Union, on the work of an artist:
"His work is all homage," you said, "but I would never call
     it stealing."

I remember your laugh—half-chuckle, half swoon—
speaking of your many loves;
and how you dressed, always a shirt and tie, those
     cranberry loafers worn down
from your calendar of days, always
filled with things you had to do—parties, or "fetes" as you
     called them.

The last time we met was a few years later
both of us quiet with thoughts of

          what was in the news.

It was night, and we did not have much time.

I moved away; you did too. Like we all do, we lost touch.
Not much of anything seemed new again,
and I did not know where to find you.

I'd asked a friend some years later
"Whatever happened to Tim?" finding out the hard way
     that you were gone.

He gave me a copy of your last book of poems—words from

the edge of your hospital bed.
As I read, it all just hit me; I cried, not at your death—

but at the loss of something I still couldn't name.

I missed how your poems knocked us around, as
we, the living, sought out sex,
imbibed, gossiped, failed at love, paid the rent, and wailed.

"One can never be too careful—but careful is not
an art," you'd said.

Entre nous, dear Tim,
the world was never too careful, or artful, after you;
and for me, it never was again.

TV Guide

for John Wieners (1934-2002)

As the '60s unfolded like a peacock's tail, one
chubby sissy-boy with braces
and a butch cut his father gave him monthly found
heaven in the check-
out lane, a slim book, not *The* Book: a timetable
of stars that studded his nights,
a catalog of lust the Greeks and Romans
would have applauded. This—
let's get this straight—was long before skin-tight
black leather at rock concerts,
before glam and crack and AIDS, at the pinnacle
of Ed Sullivan, Red Skelton,
Perry Mason, and Dennis the Menace, when "boob
tube" had nothing to do
with the T of T & A and the remote control was
still a sci-fi fantasy.

What a tug he felt as dreamboats dazzled
him from their programmed
time slots on ABC, CBS, NBC. (All those Bs
and Cs—just like his report
card.) Sunday: Johnny Yuma 9:00. Monday: Sandy
Winfield 8:30. Tuesday: Doby
Gillis 8:30. Wednesday: Flint McCullough
7:30. Thursday, he cracked
his books for Friday's predictable quizzes, but
Friday night was a double
whammy of brawn: Rowdy Yates 7:30 then
Buzz Murdock an hour later.
Saturday offered nothing like a star-studded
show: Welk, grandma's favorite,
and then local news: a dry night. So it went, page

by page, a timed daisy chain
of muscle, beautiful teeth, and perfect hair,
the softest of soft porn—sweaty
chests, tight jeans—a heaven of fantasies brief
as a breath, as a heartbeat,
who bare-chested and sweaty, sidetracked him from
the laugh-track of so many bullies'
hate (ambushes in the halls, locker rooms, and toilets
of Prather Jr. High
School), who kept the razor's edge from his wrist
and the noose from his neck.

The Straight Boy Hug

for Jack Spicer (1925-1965)

Something about holding
a man against them,
their arms circled around him—
nipple to nipple, dick to

dick—that makes a straight
boy pat you on the back
with one or the other hand
once, twice, three times,

as many as it takes to turn
intimacy to disparity
or to *something* meant to clear
a path or raise a wall

between his flesh and yours,
even if he and you are brothers
or friends since grade school,
and perhaps more so then

because time's a bond as
unquestionable as it is eternal,
as taut, as unyielding as a lover's
whisper or a lover's groan.

Lullaby

for Dunstan Thompson (1918-1975)

Body parts washed up on shore: two
hands, a leg, a chunk of a right buttock,
bleached as white as a mannequin.

The little dog who found them
while taking a shit was a terrier—
Jack Russell, someone said—named Sally.

Her owner was a gay man whose lover
had left him the night before for a younger
man with a glass eye and luscious lips.

His ex owned his own businesses
on the mainland, stocks, imports, a not-
for-profit. No one really knew,

but he was on a cruise, Baltimore/Jamaica/
Miami. His ex's new boyfriend
couldn't take the time off. A hairdresser

who owned his own shop, Curl Up 'n'
Dye, was on 24/7, especially since
his ex, Sean, took off for Paris with his

sister's fiancée, Jack, in tow. (Oh, don't ask!)
It's tragic, the way her own brother
confused Jack, made him doubt his love

for her, then seduced him the night of his
bachelor's party right in front of Ted, his best
man and captain of the football team that

they both had once played on. In Paris, Jack
described to Sean how he and Ted took
hours showering after games,

share the same cheerleader after the last touch
down, and later fell into a drunken heap
in the same bed, waking snared by the sheets

and in one another's arms. But they never
did anything. Honest, Sean. Nothing. I wanted to,
he'd finally admit, but nothing. Never.

And Sean would drift off to his high-school
days, the Jesuits and the homework,
the brilliance of some, the lust of others.

Mary Magdalene—now that was a story
that spoke to him, and in volumes.
Hair. Whore. He understood the brush

of hair and the taste, the smell, the caress of
sex, how it all tangled into one knot.
He understood being on his knees in front

of a man, like Bill, who was twenty years
older but in shape, and in charge of a crew,
a cruise captain for family adventures.

Under skies as blue as the ocean, Bill
captained the ship, called (in turns) couples
to his table then crewmen to his bed until

Allen, one of his sailors, in his early twenties,
came to the steering house, broke down
in a vale of tears. Something about a broken

promise and a broken heart. His? Someone
else's? Allen was never clear, but later, the buzz
of the intercom stopped his heart. "Man overboard,"

a voice through static said. *"Man overboard,"*
he stuttered again. Bill ordered a dingy into
waves that roiled like a nest of snakes, but

night had fallen, and the ship's search lights didn't
help in the rough seas. Half an hour later, he
called it quits, radioed in his latitude and longitude,

and the names of the familiar constellations
overhead who laughed and laughed because they
knew, perfectly well, what was coming.

Gaudy Boy

"afflicted with joy"
—Arthur Yap (1943-2006)

Because you smell good. Because you spell éclat
as tear to pieces. Because gaudy means originally
delightful, as in annual college feasts (*British*),
the largest ornamental bead in a rosary, a jest.

Or else it means a yellow dye from dyer's rocket.
Because in your turnout, one cold night in Leeds,
Arthur pricks you out and in the moon's half-light
in fear of the ear of night and of the eye of day,

but mostly of the cellar of your heart, coal scuttle,
and we who think we are in the clear, fiercely free
of prayer, smell, and fear, we who justify ourselves,
dare to take pity on you, soluble crossword puzzle,

we read the *Times* and Arthur in parti-colored dress
and o yes, o well, the joke has always been on us.

A Nightclub South of Market

written after Allen Ginsberg's
"A Supermarket in California"
upon his death (1926-1997)

What thoughts I have of you tonight, Allen Ginsberg, for I walked through the deserted streets of North Beach musing on the Beats and despairing that I've arrived 30 years too late, looking still for the full moon hidden in the fog.

In my lonely fatigue, and wondering about love and connection, I ambled downtown and further still in the empty hours long after midnight, into a neon pulsating nightclub south of market, dreaming of your enumerations! Wondering where the best minds, the best hearts, the best souls of my generation have gone.

Could they be here? And among such outfits! What lime green polyester and baggy pants dragging through the dust! Whole cliques with multi-colored hair! A dance floor full of sweating gym queens in baseball caps and tight little shorts! Wispy-goateed waifs on Ecstasy! Young boys pierced and tattooed, so young and modern they've grown ancient and primitive, confounding time!—and you Allen, what's that smile on your face as you watch them? What magnificent imaginings of hard-cocked liberation and swinging scrotums, what thrills abound in the exploding Buddha realms of your mind, cock-full and cum-slippery, bursting with boys and men locked tongue-in-tongue as penis-joy is launched one upon the other.

I saw you, Allen Ginsberg, boyfriend-less, lonely old troll, leaning in the blacklight among the meek and muscle-less and eyeing the shirtless adonises, their gentle, thin lines of hair that swagger downward below their navels.

I heard you asking questions of each: Where do you

scavenge such clothes? How much time do you spend at the gym? What are you trying to tell me with those green ink images dyed upon your skin? Are you my Angel?

I wandered in and out of the brilliant squirming mass of bodies following you, and followed in my imagination by Walt Whitman, James Broughton, and Antler, lonely ecstatic poets all.

We strode through the seething, spermy crowd together in our solitary fancy tasting armpits, possessing every musty, hungry asshole, licking nipples and hairless flanks, feeling some boys calves resting on our shoulders as we roll together like the sea and its tides, and hearing each and every boy and man's orgasming whimpers and cries—poets of cock-play all.

Where are we going, Allen Ginsberg? The doors never close here, but you are leaving. Which way does your beard point tonight?

(I touch your books and touch myself, dreaming of our lonely odyssey in the nightclub and feel absurd.)

Will we walk all night through solitary streets? The eaves of warehouses add shade to moon shadow, lights out in houses, cafes and stores, we'll both be lonely.

Will we stroll dreaming of the lost America of love? The lost youth of boyhood dreams of ecstatic unions, the elusive transmissions of teachings through cocks and male love? —as we pass the shattered windows of broken-into cars and heaps of homeless souls hiding from the wind.

Ah, dear father, graybeard, lonely old courage-teacher, clown and boy of song, what America do you leave behind and which do you look forward into? What reincarnated infant are you now, a baby of Dharma, born with its heart outside its body, struggling to breathe and longing to love. The Buddha said that an angry man will be born into anger, a quiet one into peace, and a man singing will be born into song.

Grant me now the strength and spirit to honor your soul with my own humble musical words, oh Bodhisattva, who I know has returned to teach us once more about love.

Young Gods

for Constantine Cavafy (1863-1933)

In my 50s I return to Cavafy
Who'd whispered to me in my youth:
Praise them
Boys I longed for in cafes

So I wrote poems about them—the Boy with the Pouting
    Lip,
He with Oven Mitts for Hands, the Strapping Lad, Our Lady
    of Profound Male Beauty
A catalog of the attributes of the Gods
Their scruffed chins
And soulful eyes
I was especially fond of knees and shoulders
The oversized bolts
In the architecture of Adonis

I took the wrench of my desire
To the bolts of many of them
Took them apart to see what was inside
Always seed

And the fields of flowers that sometimes bloomed

Now I've grown older
As has my longing
My bolts gone rusty
It's easier to use a ratchet

And their youthful beauty makes me sad
For it will follow my own
Down the forest path
And through the final desert
Dimming and withering to dust

Gods are not like wine
They don't age well

A humble sigh
—Well, that is a Godlike sentiment too
that comes only with age
And so, still and forever,
Cavafy's whisper remains the same:
Praise them

TREBOR HEALEY

Mezcal

after Edward Lacey (1938-1995)

He'd worked Zaragosa Street in his youth
And then the gringoes started coming
Looking for mushrooms
The ancient
God
Or maybe just uncut brown cock

I was no different
Except that I was
I'd come looking for mezcal
And companionship
And met him by chance
In the Parque Llano
His bloodshot eyes
He was still young
But he'd lived a dozen lives

I propositioned him
He said he'd long since stopped having sex with men
I asked him what he knew about the local mezcal
"Everything" he answered
The right question

We went up to his village
Where he showed me the agave *Angustifolia*
We ended up at his mother's
Where we sipped its fermented nectar
With guajalote and mole and crickets

He took me outside
And led me into the forest
Took off his clothes

He told me I was like a lot of them
But different
That most men
Were like the "piña" of the agave
The hard heart
It took work to get its fruit

I tried to make it easy
Ravishing his brown stalky body
Until he gave me its fruit

His sperm tasted smoky like mezcal

He told me he couldn't see me again
But he let me stay the night
And held me
Next morning, he showed me to the highway where I could
    hitch a ride
Told me "hasta luego"
But there'd be no "luego"

His name was Gustavo

PATRICK DONNELLY

Lorca's Lips

for Federico García Lorca (1898-1936)

Clumsy, coarse of feature, it is said.
One leg shorter than the other.

Liar, about works he intended to compose,
which he said were almost finished.

Which he hadn't even begun (like me,
spiller of seed, waster of his little time).

In mirrored cafes and at piano keyboards
gossiper, debater, uncombed, untied.

Carnal clown, answering the door in underpants,
Luis Cernuda naked on the daybed, explaining

"We were doing tumbling exercises."
Mooch, living pampered off Papá,

until in '31 he put on his blue overalls,
making from nothing a theater of the people,

sensuous, narrative, a school for
weeping and laughing,

like passing a consecrated host
from one mouth to another and another forever.

Weeper, who, told he'd be shot that day,
asked the guard "Will I be damned?"

(Whose bones they've never yet found, digging
under the olives at Fuente Grande.)

Truant, mystical, timid, pompous, distracted, kind.
His delicate moles,

the mourning cap of his hair
descending always to a peak.

Oh Lorca, you restless, lazy *maricón*, get up
suddenly and press the lips

of your shallow grave to mine.

ATSUSUKE TANAKA

Get Your Filthy Hands Off My Desert

for William S. Burroughs (1914-1997)
and his translator, the poet Nobuo Ayukawa (1920-1988)

There are cruising spots all through the city
Spots where men gather seeking the darkness of night
Aoi Park is especially well known in Kyoto
Men walk there, feet on the ground, completely absorbed
Trees and bushes watch their activities
Men worshipping one another like religion
Sometimes whispering to one another
Of subway toilets or porno theaters
The places might differ, but the activities are the same
It amuses me how similar they are
I often went to Aoi Park when I was young
As I grow older, I become the landscape
There is a bronze statue in the park
That begins to move at night
They say in the old days
It walked during daytime too
The Kamo River flows by
Sucking in the men's voices like sand
I toss my cigarette butt in the river
Wanting to throw stones at all the pasts
At all the men who have come and gone
There are lots of ghosts here
Including the one who just went by
In the dark, shadows kneel before shadows
Shadows piled on shadows forming ampersands
There are those who watch in the bushes
As they hide alongside the ghosts
Lie down on the bench and hands stretch from all sides
I went once when I was thirty
And a young man told me
He had no need for old men

Do the trees and bushes still remember
The whispers and panting of all the men?
Does the bench still remember
The warmth of their bodies and
The movements of their intermingled hands?
One boy told me his first experience was with his dog
I left when I heard him say that
Sometimes a pubic hair got stuck in my teeth
The unpleasant feeling of hair on one's tongue
Lots of couples came
And watched me, the landscape
Men who embrace one another's shoulders
Rub one another's tummies and worship
Exchanging foul-smelling kisses in the dark
I have many memories of Aoi Park
There were moonless evenings
There were moonlit evenings
When the rain comes
The first drop wipes away
The entire landscape
That's right
Thanks
This is all about us

(Translated by Jeffrey Angles)

Definition

after "A Noiseless Patient Spider"
by Walt Whitman (1819-1892)

Through a broken windshield, a hurricane whips across the topography of a young man's face. The erosion is faster than the other passengers anticipated as the dewy hill becomes a crag. It is beautiful to watch the process of definition. The winds stop. His cheekbones are now promontories from which spiders launch forth filament, filament, filament seeking only to connect.

(_*_)

after "Sonnet du Trou du Cul"
by Arthur Rimbaud (1854-1891)
and Paul Verlaine (1844-1896)

The asterisk hides behind the eight. But knowingly it savors itself the star, the addendum, the exception behind an upturned infinity. Limited and prime. But sandwiched between parentheses and underscores, it becomes the dark and wrinkled violet, nestled in moss, crying lustful filaments of milk. Canaan's miracle of pleasure. Canaan's miracle of being.

Queer Artist Haiku

after Derek Jarman (1942-1994)

Pixellated light
and storm, the stress of body
and soul in love, gay

movies of hungry
eros, face, hands, and limbs dance
the sunset music

you can't always hear,
unless you are curled in tight
to its subtle waves.

You can't be certain,
never know where passion leads
inside your cottage

or your greedy self.
Being queer is a passion
in itself, a hive

of bees preparing
to die for honey, the heart
in squall or wind chimes,

your skin papyrus
on which you leave testament
of the eyes and mouth.

When you create art
you can be alone, like string
broken and forlorn,

but, oh, images
that mesmerize the cold eye:
a young man dancing

around a hanging
boy whose tongue is the black death
and in his hands, cards

to buy the future,
flash and mock with a grim jest.
Young men in a tub,

toy with each other,
evoking their boyhood selves
in a spy window,

pour water as time
crawls grimly on bruised knees
over the shingle.

The gay singer sings,
oblivious to wasteland—
the silent raven,

the hooded figure
moving prophetically
over acid ground

who hears the tango
swirling around the dancer,
as naked bodies

spark against the rock,
flesh striking stone, flame-bearing
figures in your dream.

KEITH GAREBIAN

Is it victim-art—
the male transvestite's stoning,
the tarred and feathered

gagged and trussed-up man,
captive to hyena taunts
of rabid fascists?

High-booted stamping
feet, leather cries of lashes,
hymns in the background,

the blood-red landscape,
the sky pierced and torn, the sea
swarming, men burrow

deep to hide their shame,
unborn generations bound
to parallel crimes.

The world turns and moves
its fingers tracing circles
on the rims of cups

in a silent trance,
a blue light shrouding lovers
lets all pass from us.

Art, the last supper
at time's long, cold wood table,
is cold and dying.

We too die silent,
hands unlinked, so cold, cold, cold,
but you sing the song

of an old garden
and all its vanished pleasures,
pulling the slow bow

across a cello,
making music float in blue
half-light, the small star

of our world brimming
with the unsayable notes
of brave, lost causes.

James Schuyler

(1923-1991)

I went to his sixty-sixth birthday
dinner: sixteen years ago this past
November. I remember that it was at
Chelsea Central (his favorite restaurant:
great steaks) on 10th Avenue, and
that Ashbery was there, and a few
others, including Joe, impeccably
dressed and gracious, who picked up
what must have been (I thought
at the time) an exorbitant bill.

I remember him saying more than
once, "Joe always picks up the bill,"
then smiling a slightly wicked smile.

Sitting with him (those excruciating
silences!) in his room at the Chelsea,
my eyes would wander from his book-
shelves (*The Portrait of a Lady* stood out)
to the pan of water on the radiator
to the records strewn on the floor
to some scraggly plants (ivy? herbs?)
in ceramic pots at the base of the French
doors that opened to the balcony and
balustrade and sound of traffic on 23rd
Street six floors below. He read me
"White Boat, Blue Boat" shortly after he
wrote it, and a poem about Brook Benton
singing "Rainy Night in Georgia" that
didn't make it into his *Last Poems*, though
I remember thinking it beautiful. He
complained, in a letter to Tom, about
how much I smoked, and how emotional

I'd get during movies: he must have been
referring to *Field of Dreams* (he had a yen
for Kevin Costner). When he took me
to see *L'Atalante*, a film he loved, I was
bored. Once, we took the subway (he
hadn't ridden it in years) to the Frick;
I remember admiring Romney's Lady
Hamilton. It hurt that he didn't invite
me to the dinner after his Dia reading
or to the reception after his reading at the
92nd Street Y, though he did, at the latter,
read "Mood Indigo," dedicated to me.
When he said my name from the stage,
Joan and Eileen, sitting to my left, turned
and stared at me; frozen by the enormity
of the moment, I couldn't look back.
When he came to a reading I gave at
St. Mark's, Raymond impressed upon
me what an honor it was: Jimmy didn't
go to many poetry readings. What else
is there to say? That when I visited him
at St. Vincent's the day before he died
Darragh said, "He likes to hear gossip."
So I said, "Eileen and I are talking again."
That at his funeral I sat alone (Ira couldn't
come); that that was the loneliest feeling
in the world. That afterwards Doug said,
"You look so sad." How should I have
looked, Doug! And that a year after he
died, I dreamt I saw him in the lobby of
the Chelsea Hotel. He was wearing a
hospital shift and seemed to have no
muscle control over his face—like in inten-
sive care after his stroke. He saw me
and said, "It's nice to see some familiar
faces." I approached him, but he
disappeared.

DAVID TRINIDAD

Joe

Joe Brainard (1942-1994)

When you came to a dinner party at
Ira's and my loft, you brought
a lemon tart. Elaine remembers
this, I don't. You once said
"You can't beat meat, potatoes
and a green vegetable"
but not to me: Jimmy quotes
you in one of his uncollected poems,
"Within the Dome." And calls you
"the great Joe Brainard"
(which indeed you were). I was
well aware of that as I sat
across from you in a dim restaurant
in Tribeca—the first time, though
I'd met you six years earlier, that we
actually had a meal together.
It was such an honor to know you,
Joe, you'd think I'd remember
more about you than I do.
Friendly face. Swept-back, silvering
hair. Gold glints (lit match to
cigarette) in your round glasses.
Expensive white dress shirt
unbuttoned halfway down your
tanned (and hairy) chest. Shy
but in command, you reached for
the check. My best memories
have already gone into another poem.
How at a crowded party on
Washington Mews, during a
snowstorm, you towered over me
(I was sitting on the staircase, smoking)

and told me how attractive I looked
in my black sweater. How we
once almost had sex. "Can I
take you to dinner?" you wrote.
"And why don't you bring a
toothbrush with you and plan
on spending the night." I did
plan on it, but you caught a cold,
couldn't keep our date. And
never dropped the hint again.
How when Eileen was directing
the Poetry Project, she paired me
with Lyn Hejinian (something
perverse there). That was a tough
reading. When Alice, whom I
revered, walked in, I exclaimed,
"I'm so glad you came!" Startled,
she said, "I came to hear Lyn."
As did the majority of the audience.
My usually crowd-pleasing Supremes
poem was met with stony indifference.
Yet when I was able to look up
from my book (and that took
courage, believe me), I saw you
sitting in the middle of the room,
a broad smile across your face.
Everyone always speculated, Joe,
as to why you stopped making art—
the thought of *not* producing
inconceivable to the ambitious
throng of New York School wannabes.
Had you burnt out on speed
in the seventies? Been turned off
by the rise of commercialism in
the eighties? Or did you simply
feel (again inconceivable) that

you'd accomplished enough?
After you died, it became apparent
that this was, in fact, the case:
you left behind not one, but two
substantial bodies of work—
visual art and writing. And
produced classics in both genres—
with hardly anybody noticing.
They think only of themselves
and brag about what they do.
Your *Collected Writings*, its
powder blue dust jacket dotted
with your childlike gold stars,
is, almost twenty years after
your death, a joy to hold. Was
it a dream? Were we really friends?
I only visited you once, that I
can remember, in your loft on
Greene Street. Toward the end.
Not one bit of art on the white
walls, and next to no furniture—
had you always lived so sparely?
Nowhere to sit, let alone linger.
You weren't doing much, you said,
except reading (the novels you'd
recently devoured were stacked
near the door; I brought you
some that Ira had published),
smoking your eight (or was it
nine?) requisite cigarettes per day,
and occasionally dressing up
for dinners (which you, I'm sure,
paid for) with devoted friends.
Can one have too many of those?
You seemed to, and so, as you
weakened, dressed up even less.

To Tim Dlugos

(1950-1990)

That time you said Tom (regarding his stealing and selling
Ginsberg and Schuyler manuscripts to buy drugs)
had more reparations to make than Germany
after the war, you laughed your inimitable laugh:
self-satisfied, infectious. I sat rapt on my end of the line.
Now you're dead fifteen years, who once broke down
and confessed to Raymond, after a night at the baths,
your helpless addiction to unprotected sex. Update:
Eileen got a teaching job in San Diego. Dennis is
in Paris with a Russian boyfriend, Brad still looks thirty,
Tom is priest of a parish on Long Island. Ira and I split
up, and I left New York: teach poetry at an arts college
in the South Loop in Chicago. Turn my students
onto your work. Live north of downtown, on West
Hollywood Ave. (you'll never escape it, I can hear you
say, Hollywood is your state of mind) in Andersonville,
an old Swedish neighborhood full of gay men my age.

I'm at my computer thinking of your last days, how one
afternoon on G-9, sitting with you in awkward silence,
you asked point-blank: "Why did Dennis drop me?"
I stammered something about rivalry over a boy, afraid
to tell you, for some reason (you'd been sober many years),
that how you'd drunkenly lashed out during that rivalry
was the most accurate explanation. Then: "You've gained
    weight."
An uncharacteristically cranky moment, my friend, in an
otherwise grace-filled death. "I'll lose it," I said. And have.
Yesterday, walking home from the gym at dusk, I was
    struck
by the sky: a color you, who celebrated such nuances,
would have appreciated: Popsicle blue. Tim, I can still hear

your laugh, the closeness of your voice when you'd call,
late at night, to read a new poem or to relish the
    indiscretions
of others: "He's been crossed off guest lists I didn't know
    existed."
Nursing a ten-year crush, I was always reticent, let you—
    so smart
and so sharp—take the lead. I think I could keep up with
    you now.

Our Lady of the Serpents

after Robert Duncan (1919-1988)

In the first vision, she drew back her veil to reveal
    cleft eyes

kind

    merciful

(And once they'd unearthed Coatlicue
"the monster goddess" they declared
she be put back in the earth
immediately, not knowing
she is the earth and her son
is the sky and they won't meet here again
until the earth is rendered unto its eternity.)

Her speech was plain,
even humorous:

    By the time they found

            Medusa,   her eyes

were long gone, snakes   dead and dusty, and without all that

she was just   another   martyred woman

with a colorful backstory—perfect
            for the casual worshippers who flew
to the Oaxacan countryside, bearing offerings of

dates soaked in honey

purchased at the duty free.

Oh mother,
      I haven't forgotten your skirt
            of many snakes, or how

when I was a boy in Yugoslavia
you came each month
to scrub the mountain luminous.

 (I've always tentatively appreciated that classical depiction

they call
         "Our Lady Stepping on the Serpent,"

               not "The Serpent Flexes,
               Prepares to Strike.")

Nor have I forgotten it was also you
who came each night to tempt
me with snake
skins. *Which do you like best*,
you'd ask, trailing them one by one
over my arm like cloth samples.

(And when they made it seem   necessary to choose
the Lady or the Serpent   I demurred. I was too
     frightened to ask
"What if the Lady is the Serpent?" and besides, I doubted
     the sincerity

of the question. It seemed willful and bratty.)

The last time

      I saw her I was 29, visiting   a Romanian
      bathhouse where

      she emerged from the steam   like Persephone
      emerging from the Underworld

                      only more phallic.

      "Why   did you leave me?" I asked.   I
                            was glad to see her
                            glad for her
                            even though now

wasn't the best moment.

My boy, she said drily, cloven tongue flicking,

                    do you really want
                    me hanging around
                    all the time? Let's
                    be frank. Would you
                    be willing to get up
                    early on Saturdays to
                    go underground and
                    harvest insights? More,
                    can you honestly say
                    you wouldn't mind
                    someday winding up
                    with your face in
                    someone's shield?

Look,
you're smart
and interesting
but you don't
have the chops
for relentless
excogitation.

She had a point.

"I do lack a certain self-awareness," I admitted
                                        or would've admitted

but then
the kind of man I usually go for

      passed through
      her body
      and she   considerately
      dispersed
      into the steam

        leaving me a fistful   of dried snakeskins.

with thanks to Gloria Anzaldúa and Robert Duncan

The Science of Séance

after James Merrill (1926-1995)

Pterodactyl's scratching his ass with his tail. Pterodactyls' tails are supposed to be flaccid, but his twists and twitches, bends into shapes.

Crow's gathering the candles from the cabinets and fussily arranging them on the table. He's flustered and ungraceful. He reminds me of Piglet in Winnie the Pooh.

<u>Me</u>: Who are we calling up tonight, Crow?

Crow is positioning the candles roughly in the shape of a pentacle. He looks around for a ruler, can't find one, clicks his beak in frustration.

<u>Crow</u>: Ummmm ... maybe Kurt Cobain?

Sound effect: distant church bells.

<u>Me</u>: Seriously?

Pterodactyl splays his wings like a porn star and falls back on my waterbed.

Sound effect: a passing train, mournful.

<u>Crow</u>: (peevishly) I don't know, Michael. What about the guy from Blind Melon?

<u>Pterodactyl</u>: Louis Pasteur.

<u>Crow</u>: Louis Pasteur wasn't in Blind Melon, you dolt.

<u>Pterodactyl</u>: (introspectively) I know. He's the guy who
   made it so we can drink milk without dying.

*Crow lights the candles, whispers lines from the kaddish his
grandmother taught him.*

Sound effect: a tinkling of glass, reminiscent of wind chimes.

Pterodactyl joins the circle and we all link hands.

<u>Crow</u>: Why would we want to talk to Louis Pasteur?

<u>Pterodactyl</u>: Promise you won't laugh?

Sound effect: a spooky clap of thunder.

Sound effect: a creaking door.

Sound effect: rattling chains.

<u>Pterodactyl</u>: I, uh, might've been him in a past life.

Crossfade

In our school cafeteria where
in 1998 you can still buy Pepsi,
Crush, Tab, Mountain

Dew, Gatorade, Dr. Pepper,
for less than a dollar,
Pterodactyl opens his milk

carton like a shy, sweet
first grader and sips
through a straw. He says

it's to keep himself in strong
bones, healthy teeth, with shocks
of bright hair and smooth pink nails

he can grub up on the practice
field, but he doesn't know that
we all know he craves the taste

and texture, how it soothes
his throat, scorched from cigarettes
and screaming.

*Lights up on my empty bedroom. Where did we go? Two beats,
then ...*

A LOUD BANG!

Unknown: (offscreen) I AM LOUIS PASTEUR, AND I VANT
    TO SUCK YOUR TEAT!

A dreadful pause, then ...

Pterodactyl: (muffled) Very funny, Crow.

BLACKOUT

CHARLIE BONDHUS

New York School

after Frank O'Hara (1926-1966)

The boy whimpers through a rolled
sock, three laser-printed
photos of twentyish Frank O'Hara stuck
over his bed—bad quality,
crinkled edges; he looks impish
in one, pensive in the other,
smoldering in the third.

I bury my heel in the small
of his back. He's a Nebraska boy in Brooklyn,
reading *Lunch Poems* on his lunch break. He's got a laptop
full of work (most of it good) and an iPhone
with the latest cruising app.

Hands still bound, mouth still gagged, the boy rolls
onto his back and looks at me expectantly, his half-limp
penis twitching on his belly like a question
mark struggling to become an exclamation point.

Earlier at KGB, the featured poet read
from his book of what he called "meta-
persona" poems, meaning they were all poems
in the voices of different poets, and after doing
Frank O'Hara—which was rollicking, conversational,
and referred to a lot of Abstract Expressionists—
he talked about postmodernism
and pastiche, claiming imitation was the only
real form of expression left.

Now I fill the boy with my cock and imagine Manhattan
winking between its rivers, stars landing
on the fire escape, while over in Midtown, Frank floats
up *MoMA* escalators, pauses in front of the de Koonings,

recites Rimbaud to the Motherwells, dashes
off poems about Britney Spears
on the copier paper.

We finish and dress, and I say to him,
Frank O'Hara's overrated and
you're a cliché,
and that's why I like fucking you,
before hurrying to catch the L back to 8th.

April 11, 1861, Arrowhead

after Herman Melville (1819-1891)

I am back
from Washington. Back
to the old troubles, and troubles
there are. The poems are a pale,
unsalvageable disaster; though, like the weather,
nothing a good fire can't
take care of.
Seeing you again was
an unexpected pleasure. Of late, I have
spent too many months alone
silently drifting. I have watched no
triumphant procession massing from a sea
of blurry pages; have
floundered beneath a fading reef
of distant faces. What a delight to find
your familiar confidence
floating above me again; to find
myself lifted and warmed by your affection.

I am enclosing one of my recent
photographs. Here, rather than tamped
into a clown's guise, you will find my "Dutch-cut,"
though framed in the posture of
a mummy, no less solicitous of love.
Accept this in exchange for the lovely cards.

You have already heard
my story of wandering before
the marmoreal Piazza Navona
and my later impressions
standing before those extraordinary
treasures of the Vatican Museum.

That spectacular torso
was, beyond a doubt, my favorite.

Mr. Lincoln was charming. One might
even note subtly handsome ...
or oddly—dare I write it?—salacious.
As you suggested, I also met Ward Lamon
and John Hay, and found both
true to your description. Lamon,
though no Apollo, is indeed a husky beauty.

Thank you again both for
the lovely photographs and for all
your kindnesses in Washington. Should you
find yourself near Pittsfield,
know there is always a fire for you
at Arrowhead. Besides cigars and brandy,
you will find my pine chariot
and my whip at your disposal.
I would be happy to treat you to a drive.
We could go either up to
Greylock or, as I am more inclined,
down to Stockbridge, to Monument Mountain
and the mysterious, licentious
shade of Ice Glen. Come. I remain yours,
tinged with a certain gratitude. Herman M.

Tracking Thoreau

after Walt Whitman (1819-1892)

In 1847, Thoreau read
          parts of *The Iliad*
to the twenty-nine year old
          Canadian woodchopper
Alek Therien. He thought
          the woodsman, in
contrast to himself, to be
          as "simple as a child."

November, 1856,
          Thoreau met Whitman.
Alcott said they "circled
          each other
like wary beasts." They
          had a common
problem in Emerson.
          Whitman told Thoreau
that he would have
          an "immense
significance;"
          Thoreau, scribbled
that Whitman
          was "the greatest
democrat the world had seen."

          And, a few days after
the historical meeting,
          in one of his peculiar
fits of passion, Thoreau
          wrote, "There was
a match found for me
          at last. I fell in love
with a shrub oak."

And later: "He it is
who makes the truest use
　　　of the pine, who does not
fondle it with an axe
　　　nor tickle it with a saw,
nor stroke it with a plane,
　　　who knows whether
its heart is false without
　　　cutting into it. It is
the living spirit of the tree,
　　　not its spirit of turpentine,
with which I sympathize,
　　　and which heals my cuts.
It is immortal as I am,
　　　and perchance will go
to as high a heaven, there
　　　to tower above me still."

In 1906, Thoreau's sketch
　　　of a "phallic" fungus
was carefully omitted
　　　from an edition
of his work and the
　　　quote about the tree
was excised in 1856
　　　by *Atlantic Monthly*
because it seemed
　　　unchristian.

"I mark that brook as if I had
　　　swallowed a water snake ...
It is not in vain that I have
　　　draught. I have drunk
an arrowhead. It flows from where
　　　all the fountains rise."

And, "Perhaps some new
    red man, that is to come,
will fit me to a shaft and make
    me do his bidding."

He chose to leave
    the hum of his father's
pencil factory to admire
    birds flying
over swamps, the rippling
    of a moon on the surface
of a river; to record the world,
    silent and skeletal.
He made a sketch of an oak leaf,
    two people pillion in
a canoe joined to their reflection,
    a possible parhelion.

In the early 1960s, Walter Harding
    and Ruth Robinson Wheeler
located the missing copy
    of Thoreau's *The Iliad*.
It was in the possession
    of an unnamed
collateral descendent
    of Alek Therien. But,
it seems, the book once more
    has disappeared.

"Era Un Maricón"

after Federico García Lorca (1898-1936)

> There's a tree where the doves go to die ...
> There's a bar where the boys have stopped talking
> They've been sentenced to death by the blues.
> —Leonard Cohen, "Take this Waltz,"
> after Federico García Lorca's "Little Viennese Waltz"

Many books on the great Andalucían poet
mention that his brother-in-law,
the Republican mayor of Granada
was assassinated. What is less
often stated is that Granada had
had no mayor for many months;
because the city was so
disturbed, no one dared
to accept the dangerous position.
When Montesinos accepted it,
he was killed within ten days.

One morning, that summer, Conchita,
Federico García-Lorca's sister,
lost her thirty-five year old husband
—father of her children,
physician, politician—
to the malice of a mechanical death.

*(There's a piece that was torn from the morning
And it hangs in the Gallery of Frost.)*

Three days later, she would lose
her phenomenally talented
thirty-eight year old brother.

Federico's books were burned
in Granada's Plaza del Carmen
and were soon banned from Franco's Spain.

"Where does the body of our sweet
brother Federico García Lorca rest?"

Conchita Montesinos died
in a car accident
thirteen years before Franco,
the press only noting,
"A woman died today."

The dossier regarding Federico's death,
compiled at Franco's request,
has yet to surface.

But even before the terrible war had started
García Lorca already had the last word:
I will leave my mouth between your legs.

"One Arm"*

after Tennessee Williams (1911-1983)

Neville's shot of Elder is blue,
toned to a grainy cyan-green.

The glow of the boxer's salty skin
is cold: the milk of grain and the milk
and grain of marble. Slight blush
of pink and dove above hustling's hard edges.
A teal Caravaggio with sparring glove
instead of Morrisroe's soft-wrap cast.

Odd taste of decline and increase ...
shelter denied is its own degradation.

When love proves transient
or is refused, brutality hosts life.

The surrender diminishing us into desire,
elusively, is the self-same that raises us up.

---

* For Techtonic Theater Project's 2011 NYC production of Tennessee William's
One Arm, Serge Neville's publicity photograph of Claybourne Elder—used for
playbills and postcards—was styled with an eye to "Self Portrait with Broken
Finger, Christmas" by Mark Morrisroe, 1984.

Colloquial Poetrie

after Harold Norse (1916-2009)

i see america daily
pain & discipline, acetic aesthetic, for months of loneliness
& hard work

same struggle, same youth
emerald polo, golden chin hairs
acne & small peter framed by auburn mirror
breathless with cunning
delinquent face
i won't play the role assigned to me
i have poetry
lake silt pages to bury my fire in
at least one story above sea level
at least one saturday hour before the punch

tourist feet break the spell
of antiquity's vibrations
chronic coughing man, third shift, rousing above
this old flat already humming & shaking from
a crowded laundry
pulsations of microwaves & their false-warmth
televisions budging to Fox slews, no news reports
cracked boots with steel skeletons dragging
adults with stooped backs into beds
tufa fantasies on futon frames
"back massagers" at a discount

touch screen manuscript
clenched by maple maw
slipping down shag stairs & through broken lobby doors
outside's cold separating twitching muscle
from flushing skin, from working person

& pine lined palaces
from slivers to silver sheds where generations of car parts
    claim the floor
coffined by dull planks & pale insulation
cluttered second home
15 dollars a month
my reader heart's rib-prison

yet i pass my time
dreaming thru this
fantastic wreck
in sunset colors

ass to shack ground
i see among the oil & greasy rags & wheels & axles
the nude figure of
"Classic Frieze in a Garage"
making out in bluelight
Norse between my fingers
teasing out verse with my fat thumbs

at the mouth of a cave we make love
gay poems, love poems
olympus, giglio, paris
san francisco, the east coast
journeys to paradise
for once
i am the tourist
the heat something
i can really touch

laying together
most of that hour
remembering nothing unusual
at my work
among dead heroes & gods

HERBERT WOODWARD MARTIN

After Walt Whitman

(1819-1892)

What is lightning, my granddaughter asks?

I respond, *I do not know what lightning is:*

a bright brilliant flash of light,

the jagged finger of death,

it may be many tributaries

with a river under the sky;

the finger of God ready

to place fear on the skin

of humans for acts of disobedience;

lightning is retribution poured

into the hearts of offenders;

it is a key of sudden revelations of answers

opening the gates of eternity.

This answer will suffice for a generation.

Their descendants will start the process again.

Someone is always requiring delinquent answers.

A delinquent handkerchief is the cause of many deaths;

its purpose is to dry work from a weary face;

the sun's attention is never anchored to an identifiable
  truth,

nor the luxurious truth of an answer.

Robust Democracy

written during the events
at Tiananmen Square, Beijing in 1989
after Walt Whitman (1819-1892)

Robust Democracy—Father Whitman sang your praises
    in a young and robust America—broad shouldered,
    young, innocent America—torn by Revolution and
    civil war—healed by time, democracy and an alluring
    Frontier.
Robust Democracy—We watched you cross the Atlantic
    to aid our European Cousins settle age old disputes and
    smite evil's grip on our mother Lands then turn and
    crush fascism's grab for the pacific.
Robust Democracy—In a world torn by war, we watched
    you forgive and heal. Then we watched you grow tired.
But what is this I see—Robust Democracy in Moscow,
    Warsaw, Prague, and Beijing—
What is this we are witnessing and what does it mean?

Soldiers of the New Democracy—Sing your songs
The battle has been won—The war is over
Except in your hearts—The battle of self
The last frontier before death—The border that knows no
    survivors
The frontier where flesh has no meaning—The edge of the
    world
Where consciousness ceases to be the boat of being.

I congratulate you—you know that the world is round
But your eyes never told you that—
Your eyes tell you the world is flat—
Except for the eyes of the astronauts—
Who have seen us as God sees us—a jewel in space.
For the rest of us who walk this flat earth

These pictures are like greeting cards on our birthday—
Wishes that we might know—
Know that each moment of the day we are birthed
Know that each moment of the night
We are taken from the boat of consciousness.

Soldiers of The New Democracy—sing your songs
The battle has been won
The war is over—except in your hearts
The battle of self—the last frontier before death
The border which knows no survivors
The frontier where flesh has no meaning

The edge of the world
Where consciousness ceases to be the boat of being.
The world is flat.
When the boat of consciousness gets to the edge—it falls

You are no longer American or Palestinian, Jew or Russian,
    straight or gay, daddy or daughter, drunk or fat, Arab or
    Chinese, Black or female—

Flesh has no meaning when the world ceases to be flat.

Soldiers of the New Democracy
Sing your songs—the battle has just begun

Breaking the Spell

for Yves Lubin, aka Assotto Saint (1957-1994)

Your loud fag existence, dressed in fishnet stockings
with coiffed hair and hat with accompanying veil

red lips and shaded cheekbones, heels in one enormous
size, carrying on before us with the hint of Haitian heritage

as you enunciated each vowel, each word in outright
anger, a fierce voodoo priestess, coaxing, cajoling,

hissing out expletives and shouting down the insidiousness
of homophobia, its psychological cruelties, its violence,

its oppressive acts. Under the hot lights, you came out
a fighter for love, sweating as the makeup ran and

your mascara bled, something though of dignity in your
    manner,
the gesture of your gloved hands, mystifying as they moved

slowly garnering my attention, so that I understood
the gravitas of that moment, the necessity of standing up,

defying not only my self-inflicted pains, my doubts, my
learned polite behavior, but the need for vindication of

my younger self and all those who will come after:
the ugly, the queer, the nelly, the butch, the fat, the
    beautiful

and vain; in your performative glory, you made me for once
alive and unapologetically real—your smile, your seditious
    laugh

entreating me to drop the sweet veneer of social
    complicity;
to scream, to cackle, and fuck whomever I damn well
    please.

For Justin Chin

(1969-2015)

Asian charmer with your tattoos snaking down your arms
    and back,
disrupter of "Oriental" bullshit—

from its clichés you mixed your verse with incense and
    rage, rye
humor, and dragon's breath,

spilling forth your jeweled and jaded words—trickster or
    punk,
Genet bad boy of the East

or better yet, the screwed-up West—your home was the
    Barbary Coast—
incendiary activist, sexual

renegade, marauding corrupter from the gutter to the
    cultural heights;
your voice is as vital now

as it's ever been. No simpering verse of apology, no
    cowering, honor-
bound bow, but lyrics raw, subversive, addictive.

Rue de Seurs*

after Constantine Cavafy (1863-1933)

How simple if love could be so divided
a matter of right or left
and that merely by not choosing
one might double love's variety.
The mind has many sides
and can be as equally split,
but the heart must make
its lonely decision on its own,
demand its recompense, its pound
of flesh. For though a man be
dazzled by illusion, at morning,
when the mystery has fled,
he must confront
the harshness
of daylight; then
must he leave,
lost in a city
of regret.

* "Cavafy was an active homosexual. When he felt lonely he would search the streets for young men. On the left side of the nearby rue de Seurs female prostitutes paraded every night, the right side was reserved for male prostitutes." Elon, Amos. "The Ghost City." Article in *The New York Review of Books*. May 26, 2005. Vol. LII, No. 9. p. 46.

Dead Poet

after Tim Dlugos (1950-1990)

You wrote in a poem something
I often think about—countless encounters
with men and that with each you felt
"a kind of love." Wish I never
read that—truth hurts, love hurts—
and here's my idea of death,
which isn't a cliché, or at least
I haven't heard it (though as you
know, in this day, chances are someone's
already said it), but here goes anyway:
the dead know everything, or have the option to.
You sit up there and watch a kind of big screen
TV with billions of channels—one for each of us
bores here on earth. I'm sure you haven't
tuned into my station, but if you had
a few months ago, there I was
minding my own on a nude beach
under the harshest sun when he crossed my path
wrapped in a pink (I know) towel.
He sat down and I moved closer.
The rest, dear dead poet, is Jeffery history.
One afternoon spent naked on the highest dune,
drenched in Skin So Soft (horrible flies),
with a man so beautiful and kind
that even I had to wonder
if we'd really been there at all.
But the next day, there was his number
on a piece of scrap paper and the memory of him
placing it in my hand: "Just in case," he'd said.

Two months later: he's standing in front of me
(because I called)—his eyes so blue even
in the dark—asking "Why now?"

One can't whisper, "Because I felt
'a kind of love.'" But you know that
because you're dead, and you see clearly
how we mortals fill our lives with work, and bills
(even though we work), and daily gum care,
and the gym, and our parents who despise
everything we do, and relationships
with really good people, with marginal types,
with losers, with alternate side of the street parking,
laundry, the food shopping,
and the freakin' dishes day in and day out,
the mail, e-mail, with reading for classes
we don't like but "have to" take, reading
to stay smart, or get smart—oh yeah,
keeping up with whatever is on TV so we
don't feel out-of-it, or old, like with music,
which we love, but can't help feel pressure
from the board of directors in our head
to know and form an opinion about the video.

There I was, standing a few inches
from his confused face with nothing
to say because I'm realizing
our "kind of love" was never meant to be
expressed in person, with words, down here
on earth where we buy the truth with our lives.

JEFFERY CONWAY

Man Over Fifty

after Walt Whitman (1819-1892)

Man over fifty, my world two-thousand eighteen,
Time speeding up as I age, don't take personally,
The good news, brain isn't losing stuff or slowing down,
It's just that, well, it takes time for the forklift to travel to
    distant regions of the vast warehouse to retrieve things,
Like plaid shirts, or details of glamorous fur-swathed
    remedial reading teachers employed on behalf of young
    homos like me, strolling to temporary trailer classroom
    at the edge of Dos Caminos Elementary School's parking
    lot in the Southern California sun,
The spring light-glint in window of the poodle 9th Avenue
    skin care shop, copies of the Paris Review—acres of
    them—dangling from vintage tin ceiling,
The pastry shop down the block with one teeny-tiny cherry
    tartlet spot-lit under an immaculate glass dome,
The Amtrak ride from heaven in the quietest Quiet Car of
    all time,
Schlepping to summer cornfields of Indiana in a rental car
    full of writers with moon in Cancer for messages from
    Spirt:
Phyllis and Izzy—she rings bells, says "thank you for
    all you did for us," as Iz pinches my cheeks, dotes on
    me, promises "more joy on other side" than I can ever
    perceive,
The real poems, the internet searches used to illustrate
    the meaning of fog, ferns, Ferris Wheels, the island of
    Crete, the levels of Hell, shepherds, coon hounds, pebble-
    stones, a labyrinth,
The poems of the privacy of fading Upstate evenings, alone
    in a 19th century house that once stood in downtown
    Manhattan, was dismantled, shipped up river, and
    reassembled in Kerhonkson, New York, on a verdant
    hillside amidst one-hundred acres, where as a thirty-

something man from the city, I hide out on weekends,
avoiding adulthood, and secretly rummage through
boxes of old photographs in the attic: gay men nude in
the woods in the early eighties, looking so happy to be
free,

But I am a man over fifty, and yet I am still late teens,
sporting dark-blue coveralls, white helmet, and Devo-
esque safety glasses, dancing atop stacks of giant
cardboard boxes filled with plastic confetti in a lone
warehouse at 4:00 a.m., in Oxnard, California: a cassette
tape wears out inside my Walkman: The Cure's *Japanese
Whispers*,

In the space where one song ends and another begins, the
drone of the factory's massive machines and conveyor
belts: blobs of ABS plastic move along like words across
the screen of a vintage 1970s "reading machine," one
by one, faster and faster, until the child has reached
proficiency,

Until every supermarket in America is filled with the latest
invention: huge 2-liter soda bottles made entirely and
efficiently with ... plastic,

That branch that has to go—matter of fact—cut the whole
tree down, I do not want birds waking me in the
morning, prefer electronic chirps from my iPhone,

On TV, the positives are many: "wood floors, lots of built-
ins and charm, and a fireplace—we weren't expecting
that—and you can't beat the location, I can really
picture myself cooking in the kitchen while family and
friends hang out in the open concept great room,"

The poet steps out of the building at 21 Jones Street, into
the prosperity of an autumn morning, sly shadows form
in the folds between his eyes (he's already forty),

He watches his image flicker in the smoked glass entrance
doors of apartment buildings converted long ago from
tenements or SROs to sheet-rocked studios each housing
a single something and his requisite junk,

Against the windows of Greenwich House (once respite for
   the downtrodden—a place where Bette Davis visited to
   read a story—now a trendy pottery place for a forlorn
   artsy set), a tree (maple?) exhibits its garish red-tinted
   leaves,

He passes the butcher shop with its open cellar doors
   leaning on stacks of frozen game pie and its calico cat
   (Veronica) frozen mid-stalk—a leaf scoots across the
   cracked cement,

Hazy clouds dangle above this plank between Bleecker and
   West 4th, prophetic, their radiance is polished, Cape
   Codish,

There's no other signs of life at 7:15 a.m. on a Tuesday, in
   early November 2005, only remnants—a pile of brown
   cigarette butts in front of the Slaughtered Lamb Pub
   and the smell of freshly baked croissants coming from
   Patisserie Claude,

On TV, a book of WW poems, left on top of a toilet tank,
   dedicated in ink, unravels the shadowy empire of the
   science teacher turned meth master,

My horoscope book says this of *Taurus Sun, Aquarius
   Rising, Cancer Moon*: I'm excessively voluptuous,
   I'm impressionable to the point of foolishness, I'm
   ridiculously shy and self-conscious, my views are
   fixed and repetitious, I'm exceedingly sensual, unable
   to say "no," I have no mind of my own, my hysterical
   emotional scenes are the dread of all who associate with
   me, I have no permanent identity,

Most winter days I wake up, make my one-eyed way to the
   mirror, force the other lid up and stare: my eyes look
   like two holes burned in a blanket, my face a roadmap
   of lines, and I swear my hair has receded an inch during
   the night,

Turn on faucet, mumble *wake me when I'm dead* to my bare
   image, splash of water: obligation has replaced the idea
   of being big some day, and gee, the gift that that's okay
   today,

The past and future melt—I have collected them, the
   chunks, dumped them into "the chopper," pulverized
   them, packaged them, weighed, stenciled and stacked
   them, one atop another, like lines of verse, again and
   again,
And proceed to start a new poem in my now, tuning into
   the same frequency of nights I kissed other beautiful
   teenaged boys under blinking lights at the Odyssey
   nightclub in West Hollywood, to the blood-rush of a
   favorite New Wave song we hear,
As the universe dreams through me, man over fifty, my
   life, our world, become the poem, and this present-
   moment wonder of choosing love, miracle love, over
   fear

Winged Words

after Walt Whitman (1819-1892)

> *... tu barba llena de mariposas.*
> —Lorca

What butterflies, Walt Whitman,
Find rest in your beard?
What "straw-colored Psyches"
Sunbathe in your field?
Or dive through fine air
Above the river's breast?
Our history is your filaments
As they stir at your breath?

Does the Peacock still come
To the bush of your hair?
Or the vibrant Adonis
Still wing through your downland?
Viejo hermoso, spiritual
Walt Whitman,
I follow the trail
Of a Spanish Festoon.

Today, summer flits
On Admiral wings
And revolves in day's light
As it spins among apples;
And the lovers, wise prophet,
The old and the young,
Emerge in the streets
To worship their ripening.

We long for you still,
Resolute Walt Whitman,

Adán de sangre,
Father of our Nation,
Who posed with die-cut wings
In his most favored portrait—
Turned art into life
In the service of Eros.

Now, open winged-eyes
From the veil of sleep
And let your mind gaze
On the face of the waters
And tell us once again
Of your love for men
And the currents in their arms
As a river ... wide ... open.

Sing once again:
The body electric,
Of flesh grazing flesh
As the sun on the horizon,
Of the beautiful herbage
Of a man's still chest,
So our hands might touch sagely
With passionate wisdom.

Goodness

after Arthur Yap (1943-2006)

there is a public
shot of you, in '70,
at 27

a yarrow stalk of
a man in a white t-shirt
of yang & yang lines

this would be 4 years
before you switched singapore,
briefly, for england

46 years of
rain & cloud before i found
your work & tracked you

each step of mine but
a few steps behind your spare
& fleeting shadow

as you avoided
my eye & side-stepped into
the soggy porn show

disappeared across
the river where grinding wheels
became stepping-stones

& minded your step
as you submerged under dark
as a ga(ud)y boy

that you confessed once
in a poem & never
repeated again

you shut the door back
home, as you did here by law,
to share privacy

little is known of
the man with whom you passed your
sealed & simple life

whose death you noted
each year with a devoted
commemoration

you called him goodness
& that is probably all
we can ask of life

Written in Leeds Central Library

after Edward Carpenter (1844-1929)

It was the Northern Star that led
    him here, a site
of dark, Satanic, woollen mills;
    a quest to right
the earth and lift our mortal clay
    to more than dust.
As old as Aaron in his years,
    he came, ordained,
to show the starlight through the smog
    and man unchained.

This city, though, left him untouched:
    no blood moved through
its venous soil and so he left
    for pastures new
where peewits quilled the lucid sky
    and heather thrived
like purple prose. The millstone filled
    his soul with psalms—
"O lead me to the Rock"—and hopes
    Of bearing alms.

I hold far more in memory
    than what is stored
in archives here: the places where
    he found accord
and rooted all he held in heart,
    I knew, and so
I turn to faces of the earth
    that nurtured love—
where undercover moorland met
    the stars above:

to Merrill and to Millthorpe where
    a partnership
of joy was formed and life became
    a morning strip,
a lustral bathing in a brook,
    then sunbath on
the grass before the mind (without
    bureaucracy)
strode easily toward a green
    democracy.

Here, bread-and-butter Whitmanites
    had tastes refined
to buttermilk, and women, free
    as Eve, defined
their world with eyes that nature gave,
    not men. Love was ...
The Royal Oak ... the Tree of Life ...
    the garden's fruits ...
wherever equal comradeship
    had branch and roots.

There was a hope that Man would rise
    like Albion,
to speak the light-filled language of
    the dawning sun.
Then, having cast off culture's yarns
    and "mummydom,"
stand firm like earthly George
    on raw Mam Tor,
communing with the simple wind,
    defying law.

"If I am not on the same plane
    as lowest things
then I am nought" ... this is the view

of Ted's that springs
as I descend an ornate flight
of steps and leave
the Central Library through stiff
and heavy doors
for hustling shoppers, maze-filled streets
and life's chain stores.

The Bridge, Palm Sunday 1973

> "It avails not, time nor place—distance avails not ..."
> —Walt Whitman (1819-1892), "Crossing Brooklyn Ferry"

The bridge was a huge sentence diagram,
You and I the compound subject, moving
Toward the verb. We stopped, breathing
Balloonfuls of air, and the sun made itself felt
As a hard spray of light. Sensing an occasion,
I put my arm on your shoulder, my brother,
Old buddy; words, today, existed as actions.

The object of the pilgrimage, 110 Columbia Heights,
Where Hart Crane used to live, no longer existed—
No such number, no physical address. The only
Available tribute was to read his poem
There on the Promenade in sight of the theme.
The line moved you about the bedlamite whose shirt
Balloons as he drops into the river; much like
Crane's death, though he wasn't a "bedlamite";
A dreamer, maybe, who called on Whitman and clasped
His present hand, as if to build a bridge across time ...

We hadn't imagined randomness would lead us next
To join with the daydreamers lined up in front of
An Easter diorama of duck eggs, hatching
Behind plate glass. It was meant as sentiment—
Feathered skeletons jerking in spasms of pecking
Against resistant shell, struggling out of dim
Solitary into incandescence and gravity, and quaking
With the shock of sound and sight as though life were
A nervous disease. All who are born receive the same
Sentence—birth, death, equivalent triumphs.

Two deaf signers walked back the same but inverse way,

Fatigue making strangers of us and the afternoon
Hurt, like sunburn. Overexposure is a constant
Risk of sensation and of company. I wondered
Why we were together—is friendship imaginary?
And does imagination obscure or reveal? The ties
Always feel strange, strung along the random shared,
Following no diagram, incomplete, a bridge of suspense.

Sometimes completed things revisited still resonate.
I'm thinking about Crane's poem of the Bridge,
Grand enough to inspire disbelief and to suspend it.
The truth may lie in imagining a connection
With him or with you; with anyone able to overlook
Distance, shrug off time, on the right occasion ...
If I called him a brother—help me with this, Hart—
Who climbed toward light and sensation until the sky
Broke open to reveal an acute, perfect convergence
Before letting him fall back into error and mortality—
Would we be joined with him and the voyagers before
    him?
Would a new sentence be pronounced, a living connection
Between island and island, for a second, be made?

Was Someone Asking to See the Soul?

after Walt Whitman (1819–1892)

Look at the summer boy walking in front of you,
no shirt, with shorts and flip-flops. Focus on the back
of the ankle at the place where the tendon comes down
to form two hollowed out places at the back of the ankle.

Note the intricate architecture that makes running
    possible.
Covering skin spreads out from the river of the leg
to form a delta of toes. We long stand on two royal feet—
a king and queen with whom we make regal walks and
    jogs.

Follow the river the soul makes to its source, paddle up
the tibia and fibula pausing at the rocks of the knees
long enough to look out and discover the world from
fifteen inches above the sidewalk, an overlooked segment.

Proceed up the thigh to where it merges with the torso
and sing with joy in the arched cathedral of the chest.
The lungs a bellows, the heart a pump, the liver, stomach,
spleen and pancreas each perform in concert.

Listen for the music the soul in the body makes—steady
rhythms of pure liquids swimming from one part to
    another,
caressing life wherever moving, backward as well as forward.

DERMOT MEAGHER

Frank O'Hara and Me

(1926-1966)

"Stay off the beach at night!" we were warned
the weekend after you were run over on Fire Island.
We weren't told your name.
It wouldn't have meant much to me then.
I didn't know anything about you in 1966.

Then I read "Lana Turner."
You could've been my mother
chiding me for trying to shine.

One March afternoon in 1971
I bought your *Collected Poems*
at the NYU Bookstore off Washington Square
(where I played during the War).
The chronology noted our unmet intersections,
missteps of time and space.

You're right. We never met.

In Worcester we might have passed each other
outside of music lessons on High Street,
taught by the "Galvin Sisters" from Grafton Hill,
who became Sisters of Mercy—Gabriel, Cecilia and Barbara.
In Cambridge I drank at the Casablanca.

But, Yes, No, we never met.

Years apart we went to Saint John's
on Temple Street in "The Island,"
terra incognita to both of us.
Did Brother Anthony teach you Latin too?

Then we each went to Harvard
(me fifteen years after you).
"You'll lose your Faith," they said
and it looks like you did.

Like a puppy dog, long before I accepted
the passions that drove me,
wrapped in a towel, I chased J.J. Mitchell,
your lover-to-be, or maybe he already was,
around the locker room in the I.A.B.

I followed him out of the Adams' House dining room
and asked, "Do you have a match?"
(I knew he lived around there.)
I stalked him across the Yard in the daytime,
and around the Square at night.

J.J. didn't give me a nibble, not even a nod.
He could've brought me out easily
and presented me to the pack he hung with,
who roamed Harvard Square at night.

They told undergraduates that their roommates
were "latent homosexuals," causing a frenzy of changed
    suites.
One even had a decoy, a pretty blonde girl,
to pick up and deliver drunken football players.

I saw a handsome tall blond man from that flock,
at the eleven o'clock Mass in Saint Paul's Church
amidst the Midwestern athletes bursting out of their jackets,
elegant Latin and Sacred Heart girls under mantillas,
and neighboring respectable Irish ladies in little hats.

The Sullivan brothers, bluesuited and smiling,
passed the baskets while we all sang along

with the boys choir in Gregorian Chant.
Credo in unum Deum, Patrem omnipotentem.

You would have loved it, Frank?
You were pious at Saint John's, and knew music.
Did you jump that ship while in the Navy
before you landed in Cambridge?

Years later I met J.J. in a church basement.
By then we had many mutual friends
from college, in New York, and in the halls.
He laughed when I told him of my college boy crush,
but didn't remember my stalking—not a bit of it.
And you wouldn't remember me either.

Joe Brainard

(1942-1994)

I would have kissed him
like I was painting a blanket of pansies all over his skinny
    body.
I would have strummed the washboard stomach
that he exposed to the world even on a cold January day
revealing a torso perfected by situps (and speed, I later
    read).

The night we met I remember him reading *I Remember*
at the old Glad Day Bookstore on Bromfield Street
at Rudy Kikel's invitation for the rest of us who came out
    that chilly night.

While we hastily walked in the cold to Tremont Street
for a supper in his honor he chatted up each of us along
    the way
softly and sweetly, but keeping his distance.
He wore his jacket open; his shirt unbuttoned down to his
    belt.

In spite of the chill I was hot for him
or was it just the bravery of his exposure?

However, I was with another poet
as well as too insecure to make a move,
drop a hint, or even give him a kiss at our departure.

In those days we didn't do the kissing *Ave atque Vale*.
Our kisses meant something then.
My move would have been a hand on his thigh
under the table and then a trip to the men's room to seal
    the deal.

DERMOT MEAGHER

I remember I didn't know he was also an artist until
I saw his painting of three male Graces in Rudy's
    apartment.
Then I wanted him all over again—or at least the painting.

Prelegy

for Paul Monette (1945-1995)

i. Paul oh sparrow me

                    Paul oh sparrow me
where a silence swoops on still willow
after-wind lashes across air acknowledger
if I were prepared I'd know better to watch
sky for quiet hour reflecting awful peace
abandoning words you guide through hell
youthful a solace grasping foresight with each
book a visionary coaxed by precious life-hour
scrawling for fags outer-perpetuated-self-phobia
feeling survives through mustering action
dream always slinked in narrow vision when
your watch ends I want to dawn you keep alert
new enemies lurk warning warning you warn of
assimilationists non-gender-variant sequins betray
them to what is going on here genocide still
global sport this nightmare century builds decade
for those who remain use your voice all dead bare
us up all warn us severe jihad action is required
we're a rock displacing water realize friends
life is ragged loose ends are loose rage is
now rule inadequate health care for all is cruel
stand still to soggy spot of earth resist resist
don't let hands that would tattoo you that
would line you into their kilned version of god
don't vapor ghost away when faggot faggot look at
the faggot turn around fuck off fuck'em off dying's
the concern not wrongrightway thinkers Paul your
dying to me has been a wrench all dying to me is
the wrench a fuck over nouveau lynch with you
I bow then rise speak voice no way no way I'm still

here fuck off no way no way I'll ever I promise ever
ghost vapor away

ii. somehow some segments return

       somehow some segments return
return outward forth springs boards trains
headlong through sap up side reach for sun
instead of graves yet dug deep deep
dazzles delight yourself now every moment life
more than lifetime more than any one will ever
find silent silence equates acceptance if spring's
slapping got to un-peel grapes a voice denotes
a while longer when you're mad as hell
the Christian Reich has sought to that hole
you fit tomorrow into no sulking shadow angel
for you rush out arms flashing rage flight towards
pharmaceutical fascists while still blood colder
colder platelet by platelet by t-cell by t-cell by
et cetera more words then hem out exposeur
of the politics of hate hate the pope is but
a spread clawing pouncing ravenous
for his own still you understand faith belief fear
afterwards something is nothing as if its seams slip
Nietzsche liberals right all along Paul your grave
will engrave this DIED OF HOMOPHOBIA
KILLED BY HIS GOVERNMENT no not dead yet
still live a pawn for this Reagan experiment how
long can any suffer before sin leads us out of
into no way I'll go for that you model Romans
just keep crucifying us I'd rather suffer
than blend into your column scheme life
is what you are & even pain brings a distant
scent of living here

iii. headlong into pastoral

headlong into pastoral
choosing vocabulary tradition minute images
crawl about me yet are they troublesome how
can they carve you without history to compare
are you impossible to capture in this
thicket of summer briars hatred raised with
funeral picket picket signs screaming deserving
hell no way I'm going to allow any circling
though a hawk already glides this sky trees
with sun orange wings descending during
that time skeletal frames remain lord over
brown earth but now no green has changed
this a procession of mourners
yellow   set sun orange   mud red
falling upon some animals making way for
bed I deny this event because all absence
of autumn allows an abstinence of death
patience of a pigeon for a crumb if I choose
to tithe the beggar or not I'm done excusing
the presence of dying to that lie I'm aware
death's still not excused while I am undone
learning you my expectation is only your going
leaving into the following herd of death you've
lost two loves already in this storm
regardless if you're the pirate captain or
ship boy we're all in this together so tie
ropes tight wax up ears do not ear slant
hatred song on the sea that you've taught me
with your DA prosecutor libre voice I'm so
grateful for at sixteen raised braised my
consciousness to the distinction I must make
myself let go run into maturity or sure be
done for no matter the insults sporting my
queerness its okay I've become anyway

P. C. SCEARCE

stretched myself treebare of essentials except
my voice climaxing on the mountain with yours

I Bequeath Myself

for Bruce Noll, after Walt Whitman (1819-1892)

I was touched by Walt Whitman today.
His hands, cool as a spring, cupped
the back of my neck, drew me
toward his chest, salt-and-pepper hairs
sputtering like live wires through the vee

of a spacious muslin shirt, aromatic
with the scent of workingman, sailor,
criminal, friend of the calamus.
I was roused by the shiny cannonballs
of his eyes, their cocky come-on,

the confidence that bore down, invited
me to flout convention, assured that
the world was there for the tasting.
The plump lips emerged from a nest
of beard, forming words I'd heard

and read and quickly neglected, but these
were hooks, baited with promise,
luring me, creating a hunger for the blades
of grass lounging on his tongue,
clumped inside the pockets of his pants,

sprouting through the buttonholes of his fly
like wild green pubic hairs. I was touched
by Walt Whitman, his earthy yearning—
slugs and worms and life teeming through
the soil between his toes—and I liked it.

Hart Crane: A Cento

using first lines of Mr. Crane's poems,
after Hart Crane (1899-1932)

In the focus of the evening there is this island with
the tossing loneliness of many nights,
this tuft that thrives on saline nothingness.
Here has my salient faith annealed me.

There are no stars tonight,
so dream thy sails, O phantom bark,
you, who contain augmented tears, explosions—
insistently through sleep—a tide of voices.

Out of the seagull cries and wind,
up the chasm-walls of my bleeding heart,
the swift red flesh, a winter king
awake to the cold light.

Through torrid entrances, past icy poles,
we make our meek adjustments:
tenderness and resolution
sinuously winding through the room.

I had come all the way here from the sea.
Above the fresh ruffles of the surf,
among cocoa-nut palms of a far oasis,
forgetfulness is like a song.

Ghazal: Agha Shahid Ali to a Lover

beginning with a line from his poem "Of Light,"
after Aghi Shahid Ali (1949-2001)

At dawn you leave. The river wears its skin of light.
I won't see you again, lost to the dull grin of light.

These bedsheets, redolent with a transitory warmth.
A fickle sky and clouds glaze in the paraffin of light.

A world away from the country of my birth,
lands that have outlived the thick and thin of light.

This is when I'm most alone, a tree rooted to pebbles.
The pelt of darkness vanishes in a coffin of light.

The taste of you flounders on the tip of my tongue.
Sweat and breathlessness squandered in the backspin of
    light.

Reflections slip like kite strings through my fallow hands.
Isn't this how memory dissolves—in a dustbin of light?

Home: a scribbling on the parchment of my Agha heart.
You are a fragment erased in the adrenaline of light.

Advance Directive

after Thom Gunn (1929-2004)

I.

Arcing
   a cold light
      stilted into stillness
         how the frost claims
              the lips first
                first December

II.

The promiscuous figure
of your refusal

   N   O
Long breaths
   in between

         I watch you
           take your
           time

because I want
 you take what
     you can

    even as the unpronounceable
              takes from you

    a robbery that
    teaches you
    fear

when the nurse
comes with a rattling
paper cup

the dying fluorescent
at the end
of the hall

III.

They come

armed with
a cheap ballpoint

paper pulled out
from the printer

but you have no
orders
to give

none that your
monitor does not
already insist upon
with such
repetition
the wishes
were always already
in the well.

IV.

The air moves differently
through the

gap
in the window

and a hunch becomes
certainty

but you say you aren't
sure because
    that is what you
    assume I would
                want to hear

bedside work
    because breath itself
                is labor
                that you insist is
                    your own

but this time
the work
is in the act
    of ceding

    a hand to me
    a nod to the man
        I try not to know by name

Mênis

after Paul Monette (1945-1995)

they pricked you enough times until there was nothing left
to draw but from the remaining vein of obscenity you held
in abeyance for so long they kept claiming it was starting to
take over the whole of you like a virus like a fucking virus
that they cannot even call by a proper name other than one
conflated with a set of conditions less opportune than their
profitmaking their prescription pad that even the oracles
couldn't decipher because we are a brotherhood bound to
be kept in the dark and dying in the dark unless we break
silence like they break bodies and soon you won't be in the
streets with me and I will have to carry your wit as memory
as weapon because it was always sharper sharp enough to
cut the cosmos and grab gods by the white of their throats
damn it I tried to shake the tinnitus of that damn vitals
monitor but it is all I can hear aside from the time you told
me I was worth more than the pain that you now know
better than anyone who comes by with vases full of things
that will live longer than you and fail to comfort me when I
am left alone with them and this sheet you have imprinted
with your sigil for me to carry like a banner into war when
I have tried so long to flee from it and the graves that hold
so many of the unnamed who died alone so no more of this
life of luxury this life of pacifism because they continue to
pronounce our death but our right is refusal our right is to
survive when we were already supposed to be in the ground

The Pleasure of Fit

after Yukio Mishima (1925-1970)

Did Sebastian revel in the way the arrow
struck the skin? Sweet like fantasy escaping

the real and oozing into the space behind
the mask that doesn't breathe but sweats

like the men you used to follow into the
side streets and into the hard summer

seething hot into memory. But a thirst
compels you to entrust everything to

impermanence, a contract with loose
terms that was always already broken

but to your liking as you become quick
with life: two masks blazing

to the point of breaking even as they
take shelter in the rupture. A suspended

second of nakedness, stark in the way
temptation so often is but never admitted:

the pleasure is in the fit—
temporary and unburdened.

To a Young English Friend

after Walt Whitman (1819-1892)

I teach on Mondays, you every
Wednesday and we each sleep
Over at a friend's house, on the
Same sheets in a bed
Said to have been Walt Whitman's,
You young and straight, me old and
Queer, me as white-haired as Walt,
You with golden ringlets and a gold
Ring in your ear, as if one lock turned
Gold, solid and cold. On the lower
Night table shelf is your half-empty
Tube of ointment and my book of *Selected Stories* by
    Chekhov,
Both for sleepless nights. I think of your long
White body like silent lightning and
Knowledge-heavy head lying here
In Whitman's worn, unstarched embrace.

A Poem on My Husband's Birthday with Last Lines Regifted from Tim Dlugos

(1950-1990)

While I sleep you
    become 39
        the last year
            of the decade you found

yourself. A replay of
    the night, I dream you
        back at the sink not washing
            the dishes well—the wine

glasses still hold
    the kisses we gave
        them over a full
            bottle. I recognize

the shape of your lips
    drying on the rack,
        the shape of the poem
            you are forming out of

the dishwater, which began
    like a cloud but now is
        a bowl of rain. I put my mouth to
            the place yours once was.

It feels like a mirror,
    that cool self
        at 10 I first kissed
            to practice being a man

who would love
   his wife and his sadness; his
      future I Windexed clean.
         Practiced instead being

a man who would love
   another man. I think I am
      still practicing, but I know.
         This is how it feels.

Electric chest.

DANIEL W.K. LEE

The Rain

after Agha Shahid Ali (1949-2001)

What did you think? That Eternity overcame the rain?
Thus defeated, Lover with Beloved conspired to frame the
 rain.

The preamble concluded and madness, like Eden, bloomed.
For love's abrupt biography, the heart too took aim: the
 rain.

Of Earth's disgraced empires who waged the same error—
Romans, Mongols, Ottomans tried fatally to claim the rain.

Which clans are pardoned? Who, with grace, remains?
Surely not parties of grief who contrive to blame the rain.

Not bureaucrats of heaven, nor files of mortal prayers;
The oracle whispers: Even the Divine wavers to tame the
 rain.

Press an ear against his pillow and heed the dark refrain:
Only joy that reaps pain can—at once—maim the rain.

He tries to dull the diamond blade, tries to slow the
 slaughter—
He who tries to halt a holocaust, tries to rename the rain.

Please do not take photographs only to forget my name.
How did I perish in Memory's attic—the flame? the rain?

I finally wrote that poem for you Daniel. How does it
 begin?
"Death was a mere formality for your bones became the
 rain."

La Cocina

after Federico García Lorca (1898-1936)

Framed by Spanish eyes,
they'll eat pieces of him
like *tapas*
with coarse
mouths and wicked
tongues, planting bites
like kisses.

He'll roast in the heated
purr of R—

> back arched like
> a down-turned parenthesis

> fork fingers cleaved to
> ass, rolling nakedness
> like choice meats on
> cooking spits

> the temperature just shy
> of gourmet.

Across the ocean, he'll
lust like Lorca between
ceviche-white teeth
that'll chew his nipples
like uncured olives
while here
in his house,
bitter.

With Roger, at Jonathan and Tom's

after Jonathan Williams (1929-2008)

At dinner we drank watermelon juice and ate the produce
we'd bought that morning at the farmer's market
just down the hill in Tennessee. How easy to move
between states when you live near a border.
They'd given Roger the real bedroom because
he was their friend, long cherished.
I was given an antique bed in the middle
of the basement, next to the closet where they kept
their store of Jargon Society books, down the hall
from the hot tub. There was art everywhere.
Pieces by people whose names I knew
from art history texts and museums.
I was stunned. The first night, I couldn't sleep,
and wanted to wander around the house
and examine things up close, but Jonathan
was an old man then, used to having things just so.
My bed was a beauty: hand-carved spindles,
an heirloom quilt, and no mattress.
Just rope pulled taut under a cotton-batting pad,
authentic but punishing. As I lay in the dark
I thought about Jonathan, his place in the history
of twentieth century culture, his student days
at Black Mountain College. He was a man
who embodied his age, lived in the world
of Rauschenberg, Johns, Cage and Cunningham.
He was there when the first Happening happened,
defiantly queer and an unapologetic lover
of cigars, scotch, poetry, and beauty.
It's hard to imagine a man's place in history
when you've gotten drunk with him on the deck
overlooking Lake Eden, or seen him stumble
and fall as he walked away from the podium

after a reading. But history is made of old men
like him, fragile, human, full of flaws and wonder
and lust, before they're transformed by time's
half-truths, and turned into the perfect heroes we praise.

Famous Last Words: Oscar Wilde

(1854-1900)

> *"This wallpaper and I are fighting a duel
> to the death. Either it goes or I do."*

These were not
my true last words—
I spoke them weeks ago—
but let history
record them as such.
My public demands
as much, and I acquiesce.
I've lived and died
by the word,
the first word, the last.
My final breath will not be
a word at all, but an exhalation
of this bitter life.
There's little wit in death.
Anyone can do it.
Let me, then, leave
this realm with
a delicious silence,
broad enough to drive
every critic mad.

The Art Lovers, New York, 1900

after Marsden Hartley (1877–1943)

God is in the details, or the Devil is; whose hands are
holding whose, and how those hands may build the sacred
city of Whitman's comrades, the city of the Master's love.
All morning in imaginary mountains, Marsden sketching
vistas democratic, free of desire's dystopia. All evening
with Winslow, Jamieson, Tweedy, with letters from Horace
scattered about, blessings from the man who once kissed
Whitman's lips and there was nothing profane in that, the
way one comrade might love another, the way that love
might arch like a bridge across an immeasurable America.
Always, lessons in the morning. From Winslow's hands a
palette pregnant with pigment, brushes whorled across
paper and canvas until every possible scene is depicted,
every unforeseen lover uncovered and imagined. At night,
Marsden lies in his room, surrounded by his day's work,
listening to the traffic and the crickets. And there, just under
the sound of the cars and carriages on the street below, the
whisper of Walt's breath, his words woven into the trees,
his chant repeating

We two boys together clinging ...

Long Island Jitney Interlude

for John Ashbery (1927-2017)
and James Schuyler (1923-1991)

JA: You sound lonely. I'm sorry it's hard for you.

JS: Those last two pages were a whiney rant. I only left them in so you'd know what's going on with me.

JA: I promise I'll come visit this summer and push you around the boardwalk, where you won't need to sit on the messy sand. It's filled with nuclear particles and tiny pieces of waste that will make your skin itch anyway.

JS: Don't tell anybody, please.

JA: You'll have your chair to roll up next to an African succulent or something. JL will see you as love goddess recalling his trip to Venus. Venus, Italy.

JS: I knew the pages were dry but I sent them to *The Paris Review*.

JA: The Pimple adores you, of course. I'm calling you legacy now behind your back, only a third of the time though.

JS: People have been nice, ask me out, etc., but dinners, outings ... just too hard.

JA: Remember the many times in your life when you craved for silence and to be still.

JS: Result though is that I am totally NOT *au courant*.

JA: It's natural. You don't even know it anymore because you're *au courant* on the inside. Style has been mastered *by* you.

JS: I feel everybody is fed up with me because I am so boring.

JA: If people are talking about things too *nuevo moderno*, then they are just hiding the fact that they don't know the classics.

I Remember Joe Brainard's Cock Pics

(1942-1994)

I remember the first time I saw Joe Brainard's cock pics.
His lover Kenward kept a box and I was Kenward's
curious assistant. The cock was lovely, the photos keepers,
the sentiment a reminder things don't change much.
I've traded such with loves and lovers and strangers.
We seek revelations, and seeing Joe's cock was a revelation,
    a look

deeper into his art, somehow, his erotic art especially, a
    look
at his relationship with Kenward through printed black and
    white pics,
snapshots kept in a box on a shelf not shared with
    strangers,
though they're likely public now, sent and stored with
    Kenward's
papers at the University of California San Diego Library, so
    much
for cocksure anonymity in any age, at any age, dead or
    alive, and no secrets kept

in a world penned, painted and photographed by New York
    School poets who kept
and keep sharing each other's art and private lives for
    others to look
at and into through language and visuals. Not much
is hidden of Joe—tan crisp, cock long and thick, balls heavy
    —in these pics,
although he sports a skin-tight, tie-dyed tank top. It was
    the cool kind of strange
to realize these were all 1960s originals, photographed in
    Kenward's

Vermont bedroom. Joe's arms are crossed in front of and
    behind him. Kenward's
not the best photographer and has cropped off the top of
    Joe's head, keeping
his focus below the thick brown eyebrows, on his young
    god's goods. Joe's look
is bored and curious, a soft pout proud and pensive and
    strangely
both pornographic and poetic. Kenward's shots are amateur,
    without so much
consideration as to clean up the background. In one picture

there is laundry on the rocking chair. In another pic
Joe's sitting on the same rocking chair, his underwear
    thrown on Kenward's
bedroom floor, next to the coiled rug, where never very
    much
has been swept under. Of course I looked at Joe's cock—it
    was Joe Brainard's cock!—but I kept
seeing the whitest thing in the black and white photograph.
    I kept looking
at the briefs crumbled on the floor, knowing with the
    strangest

sensation that I'd seen the same white shape before,
    although myself no stranger
to underwear quickly tossed disrobing for a lover or to send
    a potential lover an unedited pic.
I carried the picture along Kenward's storied stairwell,
    among Joe's art, looking
for the image I knew I'd seen before, framed among
    Kenward's
collection walls. I found it: Joe's lightly penciled pair of
    crumbled paper briefs. I kept
comparing the pic with the white collage, confirming a
    photo-to-art match.

I admit to admiring Kenward's collection of Joe's cock pics,
kept undisclosed for more than 50 years, stored now I
    suppose with much
boxed material sent to UCSD. It's strange what you can find
    when you know where to look.

Walt Whitman Poses for *Bear* Magazine (1996)

(1819-1892)

It wasn't as though he'd never
posed for photographs before.
He enjoyed having his picture taken.
Matthew Brady shot a number of portraits.
It wasn't even like he'd never posed nude before.
Thomas Eakins shot a series of nude studies
and he had no problem with that.
But this felt a little different.

"Don't worry, it's not just about your dick,"
the photographer says to the Bard.
"It's about a body type and you
embody the type. So don't worry.
Still
we will need at least one good
boner shot
and one good butt shot—
you alright with that?"

The poet nods his head in the affirmative,
then, though hesitant, removes his clothes.
He hands them to Peter Doyle who, folding
them carefully, places them on a chair.
Doyle will also do the fluffing, if necessary.
Whitman is hoping for the cover,
it might help move some books:
poetry can be such a hard sell.

M. J. ARCANGELINI

Walt Whitman Attends a Bear Weekend: At the Pool (2012)
(1819-1892)

> "An unseen hand also pass'd over their bodies"
> —"Song of Myself," #11

Under an umbrella at a wrought metal poolside table
the Bard holds court in the dry August heat.
He wears a baggy swimsuit and Hawaiian shirt,
his now button bursting belly resting in his lap.
Peter Doyle sits beside him, attentive, protective.
It's been many years since the magazine spread
but his fans are loyal and there are new ones all the time
as old copies of the magazine circulate among younger
    readers
and his digitized image frequently turns up
on internet searches for bear.

He watches as men of all types and ages
splash in the cool water or float on
air mattresses in the amplified sunlight.
His eyes linger as they get in and out of the pool,
walk, talk, drink, flirt, glance over at him.
Most have some claim to being bears but
others are clearly chasers, bear hunters.
To him they are each beautiful in their own way.
He allows his eyes to caress them
as they pass before him; makes mental notes
for the poems he hopes will come later.
He thinks of how much his friend Tom Eakins
would have enjoyed all the men gathered
around the water, how he might have painted them.

"Someone told me you're a famous poet."
One of them says to him.

"Yeah, I heard that too," says another.
"Recite a poem for us."
A book is drawn out of someone's bag
and handed to him. He leafs through.
Thinking again of Eakins, Whitman begins:
"Twenty-eight young men bathe by the shore ..."

At the Market

after "At the Café Door"
by Constantine Cavafy (1863-1933)

Pushing my shopping cart around the corner
I saw him and stopped.
This baby boomer hipster market chain
seems to hire a certain type: young, but
getting older, skinny, tattooed, pierced,
bizarre haircuts or shaved heads.
Such modern primitives usually
do nothing for me,
but this one is different;
he anchors me to the spot.
Is it the beard, just unkempt
enough to promise abandon?
The shock of dark, unruly hair?
Or the way he bends over,
reaching for cans to fill the bottom shelf,
stocky backside presented toward me?
T-shirt crawling up his lower back,
beltless pants creeping down,
promising the moon.
A tuft of dark hair perched at
the top of the cleft of his ass.
No underwear apparent.
Was that a wiggle in his butt just now?
Does he feel me watching him?
I want some entry, some words to say,
to ask him, at least, how to find something.
But I already see what I want and
it's likely not available to me.
He turns then, looks up at me:
"can I help you find anything?" his
tone drenched in whatever attitude

and clothed in lowercase letters.
"Yes" I think, "a few moments of heaven."
But, in wavering words, I say: "No thanks,
I believe I've found what I want."
He turns back to his cans and I
briefly turn back to his can
before continuing down the aisle.

FELICE PICANO

In Memoriam: Wystan Hugh Auden, 1973

after W. H. Auden (1907-1973)

1.

October first:
a supermarket aisle,
myself and an old friend meet
between pre-packaged pie crusts
and dairy foods.

He's a social worker now
and enjoying it.
Two of his boys were accepted at Harvard.
He's fed on their achievements:
prouder than a father.
And what have I been doing?

I begin the three-minute précis
everyone carries for such an occasion:
The ups and downs
The hopes deferred
The dreams re-aroused;
The blond down on a pair of thighs
The angle of sun on the Big Sur range:
a life encapsulated—
worse than a lie.

Metal carts keep slinging by.
I'm caught on the tape-end of carrots.
Lots of excuse-me's.
Then he slides into the news
"Well, now that Auden's gone ..."
It's the first I'd heard
I question his facts
a little bit shocked.

His tight smile relents,
as though reading a list
—sugar, salt, cream cheese—
he piles on the details
culled from an obit that weekend.
Surely, I had seen it?

Each little fact of death
comes out shiny and clean
wrapped neat as the chopped round
he tosses into the shopping cart last.

How can you hear an era end
in the whoosh of a push-pad
supermarket door?
Whistlings in the rubber grooves,
gravely intoning, "Auden's gone"?

Auden's gone.

2.

Had to work late tonight.
Couldn't make it to the memorial services.
Didn't want to go anyway ...
A fluttering congregation
all gathered to blather sounds
they hope will come out as Requiems.

Who needs it?
I'll take the subway platform instead.
A shopping-bag lady, boozy and itching.
A black couple necking.
A man refolding his *New York Times*.
The clangor of the E Train doors closing.

They call to mind some attributes:
How he was aloof and pedantic among strangers,
seemed indifferent to issues,
experimental with his trove of ideas,
warm, curious of me—a young man
in a turtle neck sweater, sport coat I'd worn
just to re-meet him, all ardor and beard.
And how kind!

   3.

No solemn music
in uptown cathedrals
suffices ...

Ice cubes in glasses clink
chatter goes on
a prelude by Chopin hangs
wrinkling in air
a visitor passes
the anteroom doorway
wreathlets of cigarette smoke
glide by the eyes
the softness of roses
astonish.

And he
who was the uncommon mind
of the common life
and could speak of these
better than you or me—
is not.

4.

The last martini
has been shaken and tasted.

And it's dry.
Very dry now.

Skimming the Spine

after Constantine Cavafy (1863-1933)

I oversoak the plant on my bookshelf

and water brims the terra cotta base
then spills, skimming most spines,
but Cavafy takes a bath

pampered, as if after a night of pleasure
men upon men upon men

or a night of hiding
from a lover sought
unable to speak desires that would
pull him to his lips.

The damage is not ruinous.
Beautiful even.

The text block wavy from the binding
halfway out—
the gutters have wings.
The ends of lines
channel the dark streets of Alexandria,
watermarked by a double loneliness.
The delicate grit of pleasure enmeshed
in the paper, wrinkled before its time.

Pages stick together momentarily
desperate like a parting kiss.

A week later, again
I water too much
and again, Cavafy takes the hit.

The first time I might call it poetry.
The second time, I admit
I need the touch of men
beyond the damp
of words.
I no longer can be careless
tending to life.

An Avalanche, Interrupted

after Thom Gunn (1929-2004)

Fear is too filling a meal for a feast.
More wine taste than blood test, you sip, you spit.
You swallow the security you've leased.
Your body a shield, ready to remit.

Each pill a prayer, a deathless canary.
Its vigilant glare precludes the prairie.

The man with the night sweats isn't alone.
Their physiques perspiring with skin on skin
Heat only another body can bring.
On loan to himself, he feels truly known.

Each pill is practice, an affirmation
Waiting for tomorrow, now impatient.

A Poem for Actors

after John Wieners (1934-2002)

The room is filled with light
Our bodies heaving with air
We are present   in a way   no one
understands the lives we flee from

Documenting impermanence is a form of strength
This palmed love is codified among the slats where
we distil into performance: the lines alive,
transformed in utterance from the author's burden,

the audience's expectation. What this means
is our translucence, the utter destruction of days.
For this is what we are made for, that
moment of disappearance where we are done

with pretending we are not the dawn
backlighting the empty stage, the applause, now
we are your disbelief, your pause at our encroaching night

JAIME MANRIQUE

Luis Cernuda in South Hadley

after Luis Cernuda (1902-1963),
for Manuel Ulacia (1953-2001)

The dark hours of night terrors
have passed. Outside
in the Yankee dawn
everything is frozen
and it will be hours before
night fully surrenders. Outside
everything lies
in darkness and I'm thinking
of calling a friend
on a different continent
where there is still daylight,
where the hours in which we are
ventriloquists for the dead
have yielded to the clarity of day.
I'm thinking of calling a place
where wide-awake people
have shaken off
the dreams in which
I am still immersed.
All I have to do is
lift the receiver
and dial Paris, Madrid, London
—dark cities where the sun
is shining brightly—but then I remember
that Sally, Severo, and Luis
are all dead,
remember that their voices
can no longer ease
the anguish of these nights
when I am captive
to my ghosts.

Then I think
not about my distant dead,
their diluted ashes,
I think about Cernuda,
alone,
embittered
by a destroyed
dream.
Cernuda,
Here in South Hadley,
until finally
I can see him
walking down the white street.
The Second World War was over.
At first he was dumbfounded
not to find the ashen skies
and bloody rivers of Europe here
where nature was still pristine.
I also see him on winter
nights, sitting beside the fire,
reading, absorbed in his thoughts,
as heavy snowfalls block
the roads to Northampton, to Amherst
where maybe another exiled poet
lived, but especially
the road to Amherst, where Emily Dickinson
had lived a life
in which poetry
was life.
On those muted nights in South Hadley
when nothing could be heard but
the footsteps of distant
ghosts far
from any human warmth,
Cernuda learned to conquer his terror,
to strip himself bare,

until only his soul
spoke ... until one day,
like Lazarus, he sensed the heat of light,
he felt his heart beat
with the warmth of the lilacs' perfume
flowing through his veins,
and he decided to go back to the sun,
to the color of Mexico
that called to him like a siren.
With eyes
clouded so long
by the darkness of history,
by the frigid winter
nights of South Hadley
where the world was a purgatory
of white fire,
Luis Cernuda took fight.
Then, in his autumn years,
for a brief but eternal
instant, he found
love for the first time,
he wrote his best poems of passion
and died the triumphal
death of great poets.

(Translated by Margaret Sayers Peden)

Uncivil War

for Walt Whitman (1819-1892)

As you discharge, my undecorated hero, I greet you crowned
in a wig of Spanish moss, with open civil arms. I greet you robed
in live-oak bark, fringed in pine needle. I parade hands and utter joy,
raise a capitol monument to your manly lust. Your motto emblazoned:

Come, Claim, Crush.

As you withdraw, my confederate soldier, I meet you draped
in a collar of figs, each glistening, each a fat tear or a wet testicle.
I meet you brooched in magnolia, ringed with dewy jewels, shooed
in cypress slippers. I drop a scented handkerchief of unmanly musk.

The rot of my perfume curls and twists like ghostly kudzu. The riot
of our past moans like fog over a garden of tombs. The dead around us
no more dead than any living shoot. The war between us no more past
than any moving blade. A nation of two men hating each other's skin,

hating it all night long and into the morning after, hating it slow and hard
until our skin is a field of scars. A duel of angry mouths, a battalion

of fighting arms, a bed of buried wants. My captain, is this
    the mission:
kill the other man then nurse on his wounds? What's a
    soldier but a whore

for country and kind? A body bought, sold, traded,
    collateralized, a body
left uncovered, unburied, unsatisfied. You the whore and
    me the nurse,
between us no line of honor or duty or valor or purchase.
    Louisiana,
America, what is the state of our union? Broken twigs,
    turned-up roots,

branches stripped of fruit and bloom. One of our backs a
    bridge, the other
a ladder, one a man of numbers, the other of letters, one a
    black face,
the other a white mask. America, we contradict each other.
    We thrust
and counter-thrust, we lust for a kill, we long for the
    other's death.

But my comrade, we still have paths untrodden, pinks of
    love. So I
bequeath myself to you as your tongue charges my
    unmanned heart,
plunders and empties its chambers. So I cough up scarlet
    wine
and swallowed years and memory rind. As you break,
    break, break

my will, break my lie, break my constitution. As your
    military dress falls
and my drag falls too, crown, wig, robe, not a costume but
    a uniform.

Together clinging, we man up, knock back a rude magnum.
  Your body
a shield and a weapon, your chest decorated in purple
  hearts, bites and bruises,

as my arms, no longer civil, close for good. Battle over?
  Maybe. Yet the war,
manifestly, never ends. The prize is not won, the fearful
  trip is never done,
the port is abandoned, the bells are mute. Still I remain
  your man-bride in white,
your flower in May, your flag in distress, your claim, your
  curse, your crush.

MARTIN POUSSON

Proem/Proemio

for Federico García Lorca (1898-1936)

You introduce me
to my body
and the introduction
is a warm towel
on a blind man's face.

Me presentas
à mi cuerpo
y la presentation
esta una toallo tibia
en la cara de un hombre ciego.

Rimbaud's Revisions

after Arthur Rimbaud (1854-1891)

> He might have dodged his way back to Semarang through the forests and the hill country ... But since Rimbaud has stepped outside the ... web of the Dutch Colonial Army, he disappears at this point [in 1876] ...
>
> —Graham Robb, *Rimbaud*

> I've seen archipelagos of stars! and islands
> Whose delirious skies lie open to the wanderer:
> Are these the fathomless nights where you sleep and are in
>   exile,
> Million golden birds, O future strength.
>
> —Arthur Rimbaud, "The Drunken Boat" (1871)

As the smoke of Krakatoa commingles a steaming Dutch
    Prins,
Rimbaud aboard hears infinity rise in white and black;
he smells apocalypse in the night. Living
islands do not sleep
beneath endless travellers
he knows years
in Paris a fathomless child with Paul
before escape from escape before
ever forced to stay any place
but in the future
forced to imagine
and plumb and pipe freely
in verse until he flows
from Sumatra to Java
trembling on an imperial wave
of death he does not dare to scan
and so he strips again
the uniform in folds with the bones

of Java men, wraps a sarong
round his waist and walks a week
to trade his pay and a fiction
in Semarang harbor
for one wandering chief
off to a land of even darker complexion
to reform and recite.

The poetry is finished.

"O Captain! My Captain!"

after Walt Whitman (1819-1892)

with taut muscles I lay waiting
as I long to feel goose bumps
rise and quiver like ferns drenched in morning dew
wrestling with the rising sun
radiating heat, the passion we've known
once lost out of fear of rejection
folded into an oblivion of nirvana,
so here we lay beside each other
crisscrossed, a puzzle twisted
like willows bending over
to shake morning dew off goose bumped flesh
for here in solace away from men
of weapons and hate bred from fear
we embrace with muscles taut—
iron and steel have no match—
the longing wanting to fold into comfort,
comfort only one like the other can bestow,
grasping radiating heat and passion
twisted, bent, then stiffened
like one's rifle meant for war,
but here there is no war
merely passion and the sweat of men
glistening, thrusting curves of muscle
into the oblivion of nirvana.

Personals Sonnet

for Allen Ginsberg (1926-1997)

A lonely single
Looking to mingle.

Nearing middle age,
Still has youthful rage.

Am big, and quite tall;
Means no hate at all.

Wants a gal to woo,
But a guy works too.

Must have a broad mind,
And likes to be kind.

For a beginner,
We can have dinner.

If it goes from there,
Love is in the air.

Poem to Bob

for Robert Friend (1913-1998)

I must say to you, Bob,
You have such a fine knob.
That said, it is my job
To please you like a slob,
And make you throb, and throb,
Then clean you of your glob.

what makes a poem gay?

after the poem "A Dream Deferred"
by Langston Hughes (1902-1967)

does it suck on other poems' dangling participles
wet their expletives
then swallow deeply alliterations.

 hold onto explosive phonemes

(parsing them tightly)

 titillate sibilants with fricatives
split infinitives with latent desires
 get bound up by using restrictive metaphors
with a *dolce stil novo* meter
slipped into submissive clauses.

balancing gender confusion
only to over use the subjunctive

emulate
 dogs who
  lick their own indicative phrases;
urinate on firehydrant red dependent clauses
grooming paws and fetching home
unknown types of sticks.

indicatively moody

always future tense.

hoping to one day to bring Ulysses back from the plus
    perfect or
where ever.

finally to return home as a dominant clause

in a completed sentence.

GERARD SARNAT

Marianne Moore's Haiku to Allen Ginsberg, Imagined

after Allen Ginsberg (1926-1997)

Just way too much sweat,
skin, feces, sperm, saliva
odor in your work.*

---

* Nouns taken from Allen Ginsberg's poem "Night-Apple"

Why I Am Not a Straight Man

after Frank O'Hara (1926-1966)

i am not a straight man, i am a gay man.
so what? i couldn't give a lick what i am
but i am something and that's queer. fittingly,

my friend bill is straight. he tells me
about roberta's breasts whenever i see him.
he says, "i love those breasts, someday i will
suck those titties." weeks can pass,
months, even years. each time it's the
same, he burns for roberta's love bags.
limitless time is spent talking about them,
their softness, how they will feel in his hands,
his need for their perfect fullness. then one day bill
says nothing. i ask why and he says,
"i love ann's breasts now."

as for me, bill's breast talk only makes me crave
his cock. i think of it swelling his pants,
begging touch, its cheerfully salty flavor.
i think of nothing else. bill's schlong informs
my dreams, flashes between thoughts, inflates
large and strong compared to other imaginary
schlongs. for days i ponder his prick, wrangle
its generously imagined girth, dwell in
its delectability. i try forcing other thoughts—
news of the day, recipes, songs, tv shows,
childhood memories, household chores—
but nothing helps. i need bill's fuckrod and someday
it will need my mouth.

at a bar we play darts. the waitress exchanges
empties with fresh beers. "i love those breasts,"

he whispers about her. "someday i will suck those titties."
i look down at the dart in my hand, steely, smooth,
pointed at the front end, thick in the middle,
colorful flights at the back. its warm weight
and rocket shape satisfy my palm. bill gazes urgently
after the waitress who i now envy
with a profound heartache. i throw the dart,
it bounces off target, falls to the floor.
"... someday i will suck those titties,"
he repeats softly.

If I Tell You About Myself

after Walt Whitman (1819-1892)

if i tell you i mastered the way all things work
    you will have no reason to doubt me

if i tell you to expel negativity it does not mean
    engaging in positive thinking
        it means there is too much thinking

if i tell you i am rich you will trust & believe
    i am super-rich

if i tell you i have abundant aptitude
    all new forms & formats are suddenly loved & mimicked

if i tell you i have capacity more than stars in galaxies
    my inner resources grow fat & oleaginous
        and moonlight emanates from my baldness

if i tell you stories of cousins in North Dakota
    earthquakes can't stop them living
        and their deaths will stop nothing

if i tell you i am open to open-mindedness
    i am also open to greater and lesser closed-mindedness

if i show you pictures of you & me taken 10 years ago
    we will be indistinguishable from one another

if i tell you the door to dusk slowly swings open
    the windows of day will slowly lower
        and streetlights will glow orange

if i tell you letting go scares me
    a different form of control controls

if i tell you my partitions have partitions
   a midwestern corn maze smiles back at me

if i tell you i can go & do
   i can go & do
      and you should be aside me

if my husband tells you he is my husband
   he is the best husband of all husbands

if i tell you the best of myself is still waiting
   it is still calmly waiting
      beside the blue and white pansies

if i tell you my eyes are wet with crying
   all worlds become suddenly clearer and nearer

if i tell you death is all darkness and no heaven
   you will remember to water the watermelons
      and re-plant the plantings around the mailbox

if i take you to the clearest forest stream in July
   it will dissolve all your clothes
      and wash your naked body clean

if i forget my phone in your car
   you will call your mother straightaway
      but she will not answer

if i tell you where the grocery store is located
   it will glow like a radioactive isotope
      at the front of a birchbark canoe

if the shadows envelop you
   i will pull you back to me like elastic
      from that large dark room

if i tell you i am a dead fish
    i will re-join the water in the middle of the lake
        and the lake will wave back to you standing on shore

if i tell you about myself
    your search for me will stop
        exactly where I wait for you

JEFF MANN

New Orleans Ode

after Walt Whitman (1819-1892),
for Paul Willis

Once I pass'd through a populous city, imprinting my brain,
    for future use,
with its drag queens, wrought iron, Bourbon Street
    strippers; not to mention beignets, Béarnaise sauce,
    Sazeracs, seafood-stuffed eggplant, oysters en brochette,

Yet now, of all that city, I remember only a black-bearded,
    thick-chested boy I casually passed on Royal Street,
    whom, given chloroform and the stropped edges of
    psychopathy, I would have detain'd for love of him;

Day by day and night by night we might have been
    together—with tubes of lube, yards of rope, rolls of duct
    tape, frightened dark-lashed eyes and muffled moans—
    all else has long been forgotten by me, reality's a dull
    rust I patiently sand off fancy's gleaming steel.

I remember, I say, only one well-muscled and hairy captive
    who bucked passionately beneath me;

Again I ride him—we love—we sweat and come, we
    separate again;

Again he gently tugs my belly-fur with his well-bound
    hands—I must not go!

I see him panting pleading close beside me, with bruised
    hard nubs of fur-rimmed nipples, his tape-sealed lips
    sad and tremulous, murmuring for more.

Training the Enemy

after Allen Ginsberg (1926-1997)

> "America I'm putting my queer shoulder to the wheel"
> —Allen Ginsberg

Well, Appalachia, you've done it.
You've made a man of me. I'm no longer that
shy, bespectacled boy who aroused contempt
in the sternest of you, the boy who lived for
Tolkien's Middle Earth and Mary Renault's Greece,
The X-Men, The Avengers, Bonanza, and other
alternatives more appealing and heroic than
Hinton, West Virginia. Oh, I was timid, I was
polite, the sort of little gentleman my mother
wanted me to be, fit for dinner parties or idle
chat in candlelit antebellum drawing rooms.
Elderly ladies doted on me; I flattered their
twinkling arabesque brooches, their rose bushes'
hot pink. Not effeminate really, just unsure,
awkward, amorphous, sexless, another pudgy
adolescent who learned early he was no good,
nothing special at sports, and so pumped out
A's for want of more manly achievements.

Your mockery, Appalachia, made me
change. One fist upside my mouth made me
cut off high school's long hippie hair, wear
lumberjack boots and leather jackets, lift
weights. My hometown would not know me
now, my shaved head and silvered beard, furry
hard pecs, cowboy hats, tattoos, boots, rage.
Watch me shoot the redneck shit as well
as any local, puffing stogies and sipping bourbon
straight. What I read's martial, new translations
of *The Iliad, Beowulf, The Saga of the Volsungs.*

What I collect's dirks, scimitars, swords.
How's that for manly? Now do you approve?
Hell, nothing's changed except how much I hate.
Yesterday a slim queer kid told me how
half his dorm floor turned on him, how he had
to move out or bleed. America, Appalachia, my sweet
small mountain towns, I'm native here, I'm going
nowhere. It's a damn fool who makes a youth suffer,
makes a child feel wrong, then teaches that new-
honed foe how to grow tough, how to grow strong.

Coming Out to Myself

after Walt Whitman (1819-1892)

> "The man's body is sacred."
> —Walt Whitman

The paintings and photos found me:
Greek gods, at first,
then, in the pages of a play, an American one,
Marlon Brando;
next, as my sisters grew and bought *Cosmopolitan*,
its issues full of hunks.
The professorial neighbor asked us to get her mail,
including *International Male* catalogs.
And, rummaging through my father's filing cabinets,
I found a copy of *An ABZ of Love*.
Only the entry on "homosexuals, homosexuality"
     interested,
complete with drawings.
There was the picture of a man at the back of *Esquire*,
his chest furry as a shag rug.
Then from the pulpit, a minister's wry grin
and a church wall picturing the decades of male ministers
     before,
almost all the way back to the surrounding images of
     Christ.
But I worshipped a high-school English teacher,
his face bearded as a shag rug.
In class one day, he read a poem of one man's love for
     another
as casually as the wind blew through the room's open
     window
and I felt as though I'd nearly fallen out of it.
Once when the two of us were alone there at lunch,
a meeting that warmed me like the Sun,

he mentioned the trouble that might be caused by alcohol
    and sex,
a memory sandwiched by his winking at me through
    senior year more than once,
quickly as flipping to pages of favorite images to avoid
    being found out,
and intently as the stare of a strange man's handshake
one evening after a night's showing of *The Last Metro*,
not letting go after telling me his name and asking for
    mine,
me noticing in the parking lot lights that he was clean-
    shaven as Gérard Depardieu,
who my eyes had drawn close for two hours,
before I bolted and drove home as fast I could,
frantically looking in the rearview mirror,
as though the feeling of a man's hands wasn't what lay
    ahead
and the mirror's image of someone whose heart was racing
    wasn't of me.
But the winking from men and their nearness, growing
    like I was, didn't stop.
Neither did my heart.

Lorca, the Moonlight, and Me

in honor of Federico García Lorca (1898-1936)

Would that Federico walked beside me tonight.
The full moon shines so bright that the light casts day-like
    shadows.
It almost hurts the eyes to stare at the sunlighted moon.
I picture Federico standing beside me, arms lifting to the
    moon,
an Andalusian song rising from the depths of his belly.
Then—Federico's lips touching my ear—he whispers,
"I will remember this night as long as I live."

JIM WISE

My Gods

after Constantine Cavafy (1863-1933)

My gods are rougher than Cavafy's
more brutish less refined
less groomed less suited to marble
My gods must be photographed
not carved in rigid stone
My gods must be
touched in the flesh
uncaptured and pure
in their fluid virility
My gods can go
days without shaving
and love to stroll down the
street in jackboots and jeans
They never wear laurel
these days preferring
the anonymity of a knit cap
to tame their divine
crown of curls

River Tramps

after Arthur Rimbaud (1854-1891)

A river winding to forever
And a houseboat with a flat tin roof

At night I would sit topside
Drinking cheap blackberry wine
Blowing pipe smoke to signal
Watchers hiding in the stars

I would draw a pentagram on the deck
And chat with the ghost of Rimbaud
Reminding him to haunt me and
Making a date to grab dinner in the afterlife
Which would of course end up with us
Checking into some cheap dive
On the left bank of the Styx
Arguing who would get to be on top
And condom or no condom

What difference does it make
Death is a Mardi Gras
Without the masks

Walt

after Walt Whitman (1819-1892)

Not for you, Walt Whitman, the empty nothing
of the House of the Dead.
You pass through those irresistible gates at will
to sit with me on springy grass
greening wet in the sun.
You are always around, Walt.
You are my color-mad finger string
Belly-laughing that I am not alone.
You are my paternity test,
proof that I actually belong
on this incomprehensible world.
of greed and lunacy.
Gawkers point and taunt:
"What planet are you from, Freak?"
and I answer, head held high,
"This one. It's mine
and my father Walt's before me.
You can get off at the next stop."
More than any bible,
I find God in your fistful of leaves.
Your songs are stronger than any
sunbaked prophet obsessed with sin.
I hold prayer book in hand
and the cover is imprinted
with your wild raving gentle face.
You taught me every song I know.
You are not like other ghosts. Walt,
waiting on words and bindings
and circles in the dirt.
You come at will
and haunt me with truth.
You are the wild wizard who ensorcells my soul.
You are the magician who pulls me

out of your battered felt hat
into the dizzying light of the sun.

Surprise me, Walt.
Tramp me through fields,
swim me in your hidden pond,
show me how a flower smiles.
Tuck me into dreams sweet
as an unwalked road.

Not for you, Walt Whitman, the empty nothing
of the House of the Dead.
It's only a place to sleep.
Every day you rouse yourself
and take to the open road.

ROBERTO F. SANTIAGO

You, Therefore

after Reginald Shepherd (1963-2008)

When I try to remember myself before
there was you, I stand between orbits
of memory too distant to reach. And
in the time it took to surrender,
I have never been more free.
It is in the seconds that burn away,
razing me up just enough to pull you
down into—and onto—my loss
of breath. I belong wherever you are,
and hope, and dream. I give you shelter within
my trappings of skin and synapse.
All the while proclaiming you to be the sole heir
to my oscillating limbs.
Each of your words sakura still
to the rise and fall of my chest
when you finally see me
seeing you from the distance of arms.
May our story catch fire amongst limb
and freckle, and hair, and bone. Burn
ember, and writhe into whatever water
whispers wet. To quiet whim and will in
favor of wanton want in every sense we
acquiesce and evanesce the evidence
of ever since the very first days we ever spent
       togethernight forevermore.

Naitonal Winter Garden Song

after Hart Crane (1899-1932)

Self-portrait as Satan eating macarons, but calling 'em
    macaroons.
Self-portrait as Sharon Olds writing cunt over & over again
    in a notebook.
Self-portrait as that notebook.
Self-portrait as now. And when I say now, I mean right
    now.
Self-portrait as a sequence of lily-white, gutter-lilies.
Self-portrait as small metal bowl of sweaty apples.
Self-portrait as skull that may, or may not, be human.
Self-portrait in velvet, crushed blackward to blue.
Self-portrait of a naked man reading Hart Crane's "Voyages
    III."
Self-portrait as I blow him, though I'm not really into it.
Self-portrait as him enjoying me, not enjoying it.
Self-portrait covered in the sweat of two men.
Self-portrait as roiling shades of dark.
Self-portrait as boy too afraid to say anything.
Self-portrait as I had it coming.
Self-portrait as God's wrath, or plague.
Self-portrait as I was, or still am.
Self-portrait in lavender and blonde.
Self-portrait as man, or woman, or not.
Self-portrait in turquoise, as someone I don't want to be.

JOHN WHITTIER TREAT

When Whitman and Whittier Met[*]

after Walt Whitman (1819-1892),
with lines by Whitman and Whittier

His eye was beauty's powerless slave
Sit there, Thou, but not too close
To the fire. I covet its warmth.
Bereft of comrades, I am;
Thou carry your own burning embers within.

And his the ear which discard pains
Thy verse I read, or tried;
Thinking I knew it plainly enough.
Impossible to compose myself,
Thou did favor me with words never voiced.

Few guessed beneath his aspect grave
We shared two wars, the one

---

[*] John Greenleaf Whittier (1807-1892) and Walt Whitman never met, despite similarities that should have made them friends. In addition to being contemporaries in a small literary world, both were of Quaker heritage, were born and raised on unprofitable Northeast farms, and were equally bereft of much formal education. They shared an abhorrence of slavery that inspired some of their best work.

They were also lifelong bachelors. The story goes, however, that Whittier, reading his copy of Whitman's *Leaves of Grass*, threw it into the fire when he encountered "indecent passages," no doubt what is now referred to as the "Calamus poems." One Whittier biographer suggested as early as 1933 that his subject's reaction to Whitman's celebration of comradeship was "that of one *found out.*"

Whittier never came near writing poetry as frank as Whitman's, though he was the more conventionally successful poet of the time. I am a descendant of Whittier's brother—John had no issue of his own, and never claimed falsely otherwise, as did Whitman late in life—and there is family lore about him I will share. Whittier, I'm told, was charged under the alias "Frank Townsend" with suspicion of homosexual activity in 1888, though never tried for lack of evidence; and when he was buried in his hometown Amesbury, it was near the grave of Absalom Peter Brown, a Black man who is believed to have been my ancestor's closest companion.

228   L O V E J E T S

Inside ourselves, the other out.
Thou loved the Northern soldier, I the Southern slave
We two boys together clinging.

What passions strove in chains
Common lusts, not just for liberty or justice
In a time before the time of our brothers' heirs to come.
Thou and I, we might have talked, if for naught;
And now, too late, *one the other leaving.*

Infanticide

for Paul Bowles (1910-1999)

The holiday ended, to our great relief.
The structure of leisure was unnatural, imposed.
At our hotel, the stenographer was waiting,
and transcribed our message
that we would return in a fortnight, weather permitting.
We left without paying.
Our driver made a comment about the snow,
that it must bring to the dead grass
beneath it the warmth of a cotton blanket.
A black dog with a smaller
companion, perhaps its offspring, sprinted past the gate
     ahead of us,
the two of them like thick paint spatters in our periphery.

Seated in back, the stenographer nursed an infant,
singing a lullaby as the child held her breast in adoration.
My baby lies over the ocean, my baby lies over the sea.
My baby lies over the ocean, O bring back my baby to me.
The car was silent; she had nothing to transcribe,
and the two of us without communicating it understood
it was our deepest wish that the car ride would never end.
Nothing to say, nothing to write,
and nothing to feel except relief.
The holiday had ended, and we did not know
where we were going.

The infant's lips relaxed and released
their hold on the stenographer's breast.
His tiny hand clasped onto her blouse,
which was raised above the exposed chest,
and like a gallery attendant
covering a Roman bust at closing hours,
he lowered it clumsily and fell asleep.

I told the driver to stop at the next rest area.

He pulled up to a gas station
with broken windows and pumps
that had had the nozzles disconnected.
That was typical of this country.
Inside, the cash register was vacant,
but an old woman sat near the restrooms.
She leaned her elbow lazily on a claw-foot side table, on
    which rested a dish with Oriental designs.
Her expression was vacant.
I thought of her waiting outside
while I pissed into the stained toilet bowl,
and felt uneasy with my back to the door.
For a few minutes I waited,
not wishing to see her again
or tip her for just watching me enter and exit.
When I finally did walk past her, I dropped a coin
of a currency I couldn't identify into her dish,
and she nodded in acknowledgement.

There was a deli counter, also unoccupied.
Still, I looked at the menu,
I guess because I was hungry.
I heard the buzzing of flies.
My eyes grew fuzzy
as they rested upon an unfamiliar object
on the wooden countertop,
that feeling of disorientation that comes
from an optical illusion.
Eventually I perceived that the object
and the sound of flies were connected;
it was a severed goat's head,
left behind by a butcher.
Couldn't have been more than a day old.

Like a halo, the flies surrounded it, and I gazed in
　　fascination
for some time, until I remembered I'd kept the driver
　　waiting.

Back in the car, I told
the stenographer about the inside,
and she recorded it swiftly.
The infant was strapped now in a car seat.
Those were the good old days!
Just passing through the countryside,
with occasional stops to rest areas.
It seemed exciting,
the small variations from stop to stop.
Each day was just like the one before.

None of us questioned how long it would last.

A Walk in the Park

after W. H. Auden (1907-1973)

Midnight, mackerel, pearly pink,
More colors than two eyes can count,
Send my spirits soaring through
The stratosphere, astonished by

How easily last night became
Today. "Yes, the stars go out,
Like clockwork, as they always do,
At dawn." Walking off my run,

A young Marine sprints past—light speed—
Gone in a flash, like Achilles:
I was his age just yesterday,
A Mycenaean twenty-one.

Already hot as Hades—hot
Enough to make the asphalt melt—
Unflustered flowers open up:
Pale purple irises. They stand

Their ground like Spartans in the heat,
While in the shade I fight a cramp
Suddenly seizing my right foot:
Potassium depletion, plus

A partly fallen arch. O Rome,
I now know how your ruins feel!
My muscles once kept peace between
Frontiers of bone. Not anymore.

Still, I'm grateful for this bench
Rotting so conveniently

ERIC THOMAS NORRIS

Beneath an elm. I find a heart
Carved in the wood, a heart transfixed

By one of Cupid's arrows. But
The lovers' names have been destroyed,
Gouged down to human splinters in
A fit of jealous rage. Alone,

I see the vandal raise his knife,
Intending to eviscerate
All hearts within his reach. He fails.
He fails like Hate in History—

Distracted by a bird, a word,
The wind. In the United States,
Love fails us like the power sometimes.
I've seen this happen with good friends.

—for Timothy Swain

Hold These for Me

after A. E. Housman (1859-1936)

There is a cherry hung with snow
Beside a shrine, in Kyoto.

The shrine is gold, the sky is lead.
With blossoms falling overhead,

You shiver as a misty wind
Blows down a blizzard. When I grin,

You pick a petal from your coat,
Pluck another from my throat,

Kiss both, then place them in my palm.
"Hold these for me," you say. "How long?"

I ask. "Forever," you reply,
"If that's too long, until you die."

Barren cherry, or white with snow,
I think of us, in Kyoto.

The sky is lead, the shrine is gold:
Forever is what I was told.

ERIC THOMAS NORRIS

三島 由紀夫

after Yukio Mishima (1925-1970)

A drama queen, like me, you need
The scenery arranged just so:
Black rocks behind, a layer of
The brightest, whitest, coolest snow.
Naked, bronze, and muscular,
Balls cupped in a thin 褌,

You crouch in silence with 刀
Balanced lightly on your knee,
Your gaze directed past the tip.
Beyond it, there is something clean—
Surpassingly serene—that sword
Points toward, I'd kill to see.

Rapture

after Wilfred Owen (1893-1918)

A giddy feeling in his guts—a weird
And wonderful lightness of being—quickly
Overwhelmed his senses, when that shell
Exploded. With a cordite trumpet blast,

The shockwave snatched him, lifting him on high:
He heard an angel sing celestial psalms—
A voice of purity so clear Heaven
Smiled. God's mercy could not be denied.

The long road to Damascus wound through France.
"Behold, I show you a mystery:
We shall not sleep, but we shall all be changed,
In a moment, in the twinkling of an eye ..."

He hit the up-churned earth and lay for hours
Regurgitating verses to a sweet boy
Splattered—like a nightmare—everywhere,
His genitals just inches from his mouth.

The Throbbing of the Heart at That Inn

using English words and phrases
from his London notebook,
after Arthur Rimbaud (1854-1891)

Hearse — Hearse cloth — The throbbing of the heart
He would not have the heart to do it ...
It lies on my heart — I have no heart for it.
Heart break. He wept heartily.
Hedgehog — Take heed — Show us your heels ...
He helped himself to the best bit
What a helpless being ...
To fly off the hinges — Speak out, I do not take hints
I have him on the hip — Hipshot
These manners of his will — There is a hitch ...
The thing was blazed abroad and failed
You must learn to abstain from these indulgences ...
No man's face is actionable.
This maggot has no sooner set him agog, than ...
The negotiations were aground
Alright — Alluring — Alm — Almond
To walk alone — It is better to let it alone
Have you altered your exercises?
Nothing comes amiss to me ...
Do you not anticipate much pleasure
I need not apologize — Appendage ...
As you love me, do not attempt it ...
I ask nothing better than to go — To look asquint ...
They baffled all our designs
The skin bagged — What do you bait with
We always bait at that inn.

blow

after "The Wine Menagerie" by Hart Crane (1899-1932)

revives the eye / pulls vision tight whip
white tiger stripes across your back
possesses what is left of sleep prismatic
shards collecting light / jeweled
fluorescence basement / bottled / scream
expanding into sinuses / this powder
calling like a lighthouse.

Imitation granite countertop / the blade
laughs into it and cuts / a dry expanse
to claim / and drawn / a moment in the
life / erased / Blanca Regina / queen of
Siberia / your delicate hand / like time
/ wipes age into the brow / dust into
the gut / racing heart / she whispers
into insect flesh.

I see myself in the razor / drawn across
the sloping hillside / envious this ghost
/ a temperamental frost wife sloughing
into body / bleed-like / heat / into the
blood.

every room / every limit / every draft /
every dollar flown for this remorseless
sentence / letters of a signature / new
bodies cut into the snow that melts you /
beauty given accidentally to every month
lost / in between her tusks of ivory /a
rose-soft mouth of nothingness / that
blooms / to glistening of solitude / of
wanting you/ of wanting/ to give up.

Dream of that which knows / enough
to hate you back / what nameless feeds
on unknown virtue / vision of your face
enhollowed / viscera of price / extracted /
one thousand grains of sugar / rage of what
can taste its end.

If only breathing's fevered blessing / could
topple this the priceless lines of sex and spit
/ the pale tooth pressed against the jugular /
meanders after you in lines /and at the end /
you know / the dim inheritance of sand.

Mourning, my relief

after "Song of Myself" (Verses XLIV-LII)
by Walt Whitman (1819-1892)

1.

I have seen death; shadow of an airplane
like a smooth flint skipped across the surface of a field;
a field whose grass is gold with death and ripples like a
    windswept lake.
        Death, a shiver passed along the skin.
            I have seen it, just like this, since I was young:
watching from below,
    wondering about the destination of its passengers—

2.

Mourning, my relief is found and lost in you!
    I have found and lost my God within the swell and ebb
        of grief—

        We long for what is simple,
and how simple is the burden of despair—how bracing,
    how preoccupying of our hands.

3.

    no more doubt.

    no more light.

    I'm tired and I want to lie here with you in the dark.

Listen: I have sought my love and death inside the bodies
of strange men
and found them both.
Love, a length of entrail, bile sheath,
hot little factory and infinitely complex maze of impulse:
grow, nourish, blush, harm
spiral through the gut.

I've lost my way inside affection. I am too wrapped up to
move.
Love, tangled like a phone cord, like the ones my
lovers are too young to know—
but listen, something's calling.
Something is announcing itself without words.

4.

Hush, don't give me away, but come close.
Listen with me as my older brother's talking dirty
to a girl we cannot see;

It's love: our ears pressed tight against the flesh-hot plastic
of the old receiver.
Closer, closer! Lush as whisper.

Bleak as sun-stained valentine, and death, the stench of
what we are not ready to digest.

5.

Death is every bit as handsome as a boy, and I have waited
for him
in the cafeteria, watched him in the locker room,

as he arrives with track star's grace, beauty murderous and
    made
        of sinew.

His golden eyes run over me (shadow on the field! a plane!)
        But he sees nothing. Rings of sweat writhe through
           his jersey,
haloed darknesses, velocity's dank cost, the reek of animal
    come-hithering me—

Ah, Pheromone! White shirt and a fitted cap—
        Death knows I'm a sucker
           for the winking of the gold chain on his neck,
                coppered with light.
Ah, Death, come tumble with me—
                when I wake up, I'll remember you.
                I'll write for you another song.

6.

You whose grasp has fixed me to a bed, whose name slips
    in between my fingers—
Tell me how we met, how it was I came to be seduced by
    you?
        I have loved you; loved your hands; your thumb
           slipped in between my teeth.
My lips around you, here: my soft red wedding ring.
        You, whose breathing I have loved across my neck,
How I've listened to it settle as you've slept.
    The dawn is like a husband, just returning,

    I've resolved to leave but quietly.
my shorts stay hidden underneath the bed as I slip out
    your window,
first one naked leg and then another.

7.

Ah, the waste of burying myself in anything besides a
    lover's hair!
      How I dread the grave!
The earth asks only if I will allow myself to be held in its
    arms a short time—
          still, be patient, my descending sun!
Just a little longer, please, you shadows who now beckon at
    the corners of the eye!

        I cannot be gone while grief still parks his car
and taps the horn for me to bleed out of the house.
    Sorrow, never let me go.
I'm not done being shocked by you, I don't want to heal,
    don't leave!

I want to stay alive with you, living with the pain as long
    as I can bear it
and to hope the world will slow for someone as I die, like
    this:

an unseen telephone that rings sweetly with music;

a plane that never lands but rather flies directly toward a
    sun
         that hangs like the unblinking eye of death,
         unmoving in the center of the sky.

This Garden Needs Hands That Aren't Hired

*for Federico García Lorca,
murdered by Fascists (1898-1936)*

I am a flower
and my hand is my sun
that warms to life
the flower in me.
Lorca they say was
killed by Falangist bandits
with a shot up the ass for being queer.
He died
like I die
in a fertile country.

But I live again
after each petite death
of supreme forgetting:
the aloneness the dark root
of a scream.
I must make
the protein flower grow
to crush down inside me
the shriek that stands on tiptoe
waiting to remind me
that I am no one else.

I build my purl-veined harrow
of astonished flesh,
I cultivate the blood flower
of forgetting.

But my sun melts my harrow,
melts the paraffin flower
that blanches,

runs like liquid camellia,
dissolving to forgetting,
for getting the fore-gotten
sentence of aloneness.

And I wonder
what were Falangist bandits
and if they did any good
in the garden of bitter rosebay.

Photo Op at Walt Whitman Junior College
after Walt Whitman (1819-1892)

Swimmer's Bodies.
Long, lean, hard-muscled.
Water Jocks. Sun-freckled shoulders.
Chest and arms built by lap after lap
of backstroke, crawl, and butterfly.
Clean chlorine smell of pits and crotch
and sunstreaked hair.

Robed, they mill on the breezy pool edge,
toes curling, hot for competition,
28 young men on two college teams,
handing off their robes
for a test plop into the flat blue water's roped lanes.
Stretched nylon trunks, brief, pouched.
The warm assurance
of a quick self-grope.
The feel of a buddy's cupped palm
patting encouragement
on a wet nylon rump.
The swimmer's jockstrap:
lightweight, cotton banded
around muscular collegiate waist,
strapped down around symmetrical moons
of golden undergrad butt.
Grab-ass, towel-snapping
naked horseplay in the showers,
but serious at the water's edge. Intense.
Water animals.
Fresh wet hair tucked
with long-fingered hand into tight latex cap.
Bright eyes, goggled.
28 young men,
splashing and dripping with sun.

28 young men and all so ... manly.
They hardly douse
whom they know
with spray
when to cheers they raise victorious fists,
pulled triumphant from the pool,
walking barefoot past the bleachers,
leaving wet prints of perfect feet
and dripping Speedo trunks.
Eyes reach out to feel
what applauding hands may not touch.
Love's lust makes the swimmers' bodies
loved all the more.

Overhead, above their nearly naked brotherhood,
a long-muscled diver takes golden flight:
bouncing, then launched, tucked, rolled,
knifing downward through the crystal air,
slicing through sun into deep waters:
a dove breaking the surface of the sea,
a god in graceful descent,
a man in full plunging dare.
Cameras click. Telephoto touch.
All their warm wet images, single-framed,
for magical conjuring, late
in the private one-handed night.

Asphyxia by Gentrification

for Pier Paolo Pasolini (1922-1975)

Cities breathe.
Sometimes they inhale you.
Sometimes they exhale you.
Experience teaches wisdom.
I may love the city.
The city may not love me back.
Not adjusted where I am,
run down the moon,
go where my adjustment is.

Get out of Dodge,
pack up,
make my same mistakes
in another city.

Baudelaire bitterly bitched
squatting homeless:
"The form of a city
changes more quickly,
alas! than the human heart."

Clutching my pearls,
with socialist hauteur,
I decided not to buy a home.
I lost playing gay Monopoly
while my landlord spun the chamber
turning rent control into Russian roulette.

Paris grew tired
of Hemingway's Lost Generation
and found new lovers.

I been kicked out

of better places than this.
I am causing my own suffering.
As a hoarder packing up
my Buddhist art books,
I should know better.

Song for Sunrise

after Walt Whitman (1819-1892)

The one percent vanilla yogurt
I shall be you the fat free honey
yogurt I shall be you the smoke
flavored almonds the plain almonds
the salted roasted almonds I
shall be you the produce section
attristers me the khaki'd debutant
mon revenant inspecting organic
bananas with his doting mother
which of the bunch will you bag
my last breath fogs them all and
your last my foggy first all will
bruise and soften the black sapote
the ackee and its creamy poisons
the bull's heart the exocarp and
mesocarp equally bruising where
I press my disastrous tongue the
hairless rambutan and lychee
luminous as testicles the islands
will bruise and the lakes will
bruise and soften the sapodilla the
ugli fruit and sharlyn melon I am
uglier than you and uglier than all
is the stone fruit's lignified stone
I spit you into the lake where I
spit all the grateful and ungrateful
things the broken Cuisinart
blender the neck's subluxations
the clonazepam and buspar I
shall be you the tub of gelatinous
spinach I spit you out the cute
Foucauldian in the back row of

the lecture hall I spit you out the
pink sheened insomniac snake of
his loins it will bruise and soften
sunrise falling into my room like
an eavesdropper on the other side
of the door this is how it begins
the cosmic threesome it tumbles in
did you overhear something juicy I
tie my robe round the whole tear-
lashed ensemble I flash the day
my insides bursting with triste
and the day bursts as is fitting the
night bursts and noon bursts the
poacher coddling his third day eggs
swirling the vinegar the muffin
girl cursing her tin of muffins
the president with his mouth of
maggots the syphilitic rot closing
in the meal moths asleep in sacks
of flour their day will come the he-
mouse asleep in the sink and the
mouse turds dreaming under the
sink their day will come I can't
help but lash out at the he-mouse
endless bickering echo do you not
think I remember the boomgaarden
the day I woke in bed with another
man the boy who said I am lucky
and you are lucky too to whom was
he speaking I remember that luck
with its masque of tar and feathers
I plucked the feathers I wear the
tarring how it saps my interests.

To a Drag Queen Dying Young

after A. E. Housman (1859-1936)

The time you won your pearly crown
We chaired you in your scarlet gown;
Tuxedoed men lifted you on high,
A single tear formed in your eye:

A single tear against a smile
As you glided down the Nile
Resplendent in a gilded chair,
A dream now true, an answered prayer.

A father's scorn, a mother's dress
Lay behind your happiness;
A son denied, reviled and scorned,
A face that cried to be adorned.

Smart fellow, not to listen long
To Beauty's ancient siren song,
To slip away without a trace
Of disappointment on your face.

Other queens who passed their prime
And met the ravages of time
Found that youth made better sense—
Glamor is a poor defense.

We lifted you with lusty cheers
And buried you with angry tears;
Confronting grief as best we can
We mourn the woman and the man.

The memory of your stylish reign
Gives us wisdom in our pain;

DENNIS RHODES

We close your closet with the gloom
Of those who sealed Cleopatra's tomb.

Divinity

after Walt Whitman (1819-1892)

Divine are the gravel roads leading out of the Heartland.
Divine are the crisp flower-beds edging the Amish farms.
Divine are the horses, trotting through the pastoral
    morning.
Divine are the lilacs beside the farm house I am leaving.
Divine are the two hundred dollars in my wallet.
Divine is my Muse who inspired my sweetest songs.
Divine is Chicago O'Hare airport.
Divine is our parting embrace.
Divine is the Pacific.
Divine is Puna.
Divine is Kilauea volcano.
Divine is the eruption.
Divine are the black sand beaches.
Divine are the wild orchids.
Divine is his body in the moonlight.
Divine is creation.

GARY BOELHOWER

Upon Waking

after Fernando Pessoa (1888-1935)

Last night the honey bees
deposited their sweet nectar
in the small spaces of my spine
their sticky feet tickling the tendons
tensioned with knowledge and failure
their small songs echoing
into the cortical chambers prying
into the hippocampus with prisms
of light seeping into the networks
of neurons. All the work of bees
and childhood memories
songs of jonquils and daffodils
all the shades of buds and shoots
sage sap plum and sea
synapsing in the cellular entanglements
in the soft ethers of dreams.
Waking into the spring light
your body warm against my body
flooded with amber and mercy
the color and taste of honey.

Claim the Ancient Tribe

after Walt Whitman (1819-1892)

Come with me down to the water
to remove the husks
buttoned belted snapped and stitched to our bodies

remove all that comes between us
and the sun's kiss
the wind's playful fingers

bright and *common air that bathes the globe*
pollen from all the blooms of summer
mist and stardust *play of shine and shade*

down to the water
where we can be unclad and lucky
careless and *not a bit tamed*

with lush and liquid songs on our lips
lay our hands
on the hills and valleys of tenderness

the green risings *urge and urge and urge*
the roots going deep.

Let us above all be gentle
and fearless
say the words that count

claim the ancient tribe
and all the rites of our belonging
that pulse in our blood and bone.

GARY BOELHOWER

The sacrament of your sweet flesh
I take into my mouth
mercy and miracle.

Kosmic Haikus for Walt

after Walt Whitman (1819-1892)

Camerado, you
ate up all the words back then.
Are you hangry yet?

Your line spinning out,
an aria translating
American air.

Your lusty self-song!
Your firm masculine colter!
Hook-up apps melt down.

Atolls of haiku
can't contain your multitudes,
tsunami poet.

Gig economy.
No loafing, no ease allowed,
no song of ourselves.

Among leaves of grass,
virtuous reality:
arm-pits and kosmos.

This minimal form:
you'd open to the journey-
work of the stars.*

Aphrodisiac

after James L. White (1936-1981)

In Minneapolis, where you once strolled on
these streets that I walk Rocky, his tags jangling
as he investigates one more tree,
I dream of running into you, waving.

I've never met you, nor would I agree
you'd look sexy in a pornographic film:
clean-shaven, balding, fat. Not my type.
My fantasies were beyond Hollywood.

In Washington, D.C. during the '80s,
testosterone competed with my studies.
So what if I had a heartache
or two? I was an eternal hopeful.

On Friday and Saturday nights I sneaked
out to Lambda Rising, where guys commingled
prior to hitting the bars. I eyed
their bulges propped and angled for effect

as I wandered past the shelves of paperbacks,
its lurid covers showing muscular men
standing adroitly from each other,
usually shirtless against lush palm trees,

blue skies, an ocean waiting to be broken
by their bodies, at last shorn of doubt and shame,
desire a quicksilver flame between
their eyes having commanded discretion.

In Lambda Rising, no one needed to ask:
customers browsed each other openly,

glances betting against night to come.
Love? Ha. We were simply young and horny,

not seeing how soon these nights would disappear:
orgasms swallowed by fear of saliva,
suspicions of next-in-line to die,
Washington Blade filling rows of obits.

We'd soon learn how to ask if one had AIDS or
HIV, practice unfurling our condoms,
and drink away our hesitations
with booze-infused kisses of nonchalance.

Streetlamps on P Street watched us boomeranging,
eyes bright with hope and lust, praying for The One
there, glancing our way, unexpected,
always different from how we'd envisioned.

Late one night, when the bookstore was still open,
rain pelted me. Lightning flashbulbed me running
inside. I found all my clothes soaked,
outlining my flat chest, my thin ass, and

my hairy back. No wonder no one returned
my lonely glances. I had no charisma,
no designer clothes, no expensive haircuts,
no car. I was a shadow becoming.

What could be wrong with me? Was it my hearing
aids, nasal voice, stick-figure physique, freckles?
As I dried, I scanned the racks of smut,
its shiny covers demanding I peek

inside for flashes of muscular perfection,
mammoth erections framed by a wicked smile,
as if they'd seen the inevitable
reactions throbbing in my underwear.

RAYMOND LUCZAK

I ached to take home these glossy magazines,
but I was a college student. I needed
something cheaper. Below the porno
racks were lesbian and gay newspapers

from around America and Canada.
Guys standing next to me groped themselves only
to find me feigning indifference.
They looked like slim pickings at a bar's close.

How I might end up desperate like them was
a question I never wanted to ask, yet
as I picked up *The James White Review*,
I wondered if unfolding its pages would

somehow reveal my future as a gay man.
Poems and stories opened like centerfolds.
Petulant lines jumped out like hard-ons.
Buying a fresh copy felt like foreplay.

but I didn't beat off to all that I read.
That night I didn't feel lonely, knowing
some guys out in Minneapolis
had bothered putting together a journal.

I hunted down your poems. The salt of you:
"everything rises from my dick to my breath
saying we are here" pumped my veins.
What I'd experienced was beyond words.

You described how making love could be bungled.
Their bodies could never be found in blue films
that played downtown on Hennepin.
You cast pinlights into each room of night

where lawmen were arrested into silence
observing how guys, toughened like themselves,

made love: no other language but this
inchoate translation of connecting.

Listening to you, I dared myself, speaking
unspeakable lusts once footnoted in my dreams.
Sex dribbled beads of sweat down the page.
Could this be really me? What would friends think?

You wrote about this and that guy
as if it were the most ordinary thing.
I envied your casual boldness:
"Just some understanding between two men."

In the flannel sheets of my heartaches,
you, unflinching in that Midwestern manner,
sweet-healed me with twilight embraces:
"done with my memory, my cock and hands."

Impossible I should fall in love with you,
a nobody famous who was a former
dancer who taught the Navajo before moving
here in Minnesota. History says

you were only forty-five years old
when cardiovascular disease took you.
Thank God you'd died before AIDS appeared,
or you'd have been just another number.

I'm middle-aged. I'm losing hair. I have to
wear glasses when I write. I'm four years single,
but that's okay. I'll live. I still dream
good feelings that can happen between men.

On the Death of Joseph Rodman Drake, Redux
after Fitz-Greene Halleck (1790-1867)

Green be the turf above thee,

>   *This thick grass is the sweetest bed*

Friend of my better days!

>   *for the nakedness of our hairy bodies*

None knew thee but to love thee,

>   *as we shout and moan and grunt*

Nor named thee but to praise.

>   *each other's name while edging.*

Tears fell, when thou went dying,

>   *When we at last explode from ecstasy,*

From eyes unused to weep,

>   *we will weep fantastic tears of joy and laugh,*

And long where thou art lying,

>   *clinging to each other in a warm shower*

Will tears the cold turf steep.

>   *before the stars blanket us with dreams.*

When hearts, whose truth was proven,

>   *We feel goofy in our matching suits,*

Like throe, are laid in earth,

>   *but we glow when family and friends gather*

There should a wreath be woven

>   *around us like a wreath of evergreen*

To tell the world their worth;

as we proclaim our love for all time.

And I, who woke each morrow

Neighbors will know us as those guys

To clasp thy hand in mine,

who always give each other a good-bye kiss

Who shared thy joy and sorrow,

before heading off for another day at work.

Whose weal and woe were thine;

Sometimes one of us may have a quickie

It should be mine to braid it

with a hot number online, but it's not

Around thy faded brow,

a big deal. We're only guys. We understand

But I've in vain essayed it,

the need to scratch that itch now and then.

And I feel I cannot now.

We still love each other no matter what.

While memory bids me weep thee,

The day will come when one of us dies

Nor thoughts nor words are free,

much too soon. But we will never be alone

The grief is fixed too deeply

in this bright and shining world of days

That mourns a man like thee.

when no one need be ashamed to love.

Marriage

for Christopher Isherwood (1904-1986)

> "The common cormorant (or shag)
> Lays eggs inside a paper bag
> The reason you will see no doubt
> It is to keep the lightning out"
> —"The Common Cormorant"

I don't understand heterosexual marriage.
My friend is cheating on her husband.
The man she is having an affair with bakes
the most delicious bread and gave my friend
the recipe. When she was making
her husband a loaf of this adulterous bread,
her wedding ring slipped off in the dough.
When he bit into it, he chipped his tooth.
Now she feels tremendous guilt and a little pain
when she kisses him and tongues the jagged edge.
My husband kisses all the men he wants. Most
of the time, it's me. He lost his wedding ring
once. I found it three days later in the spot
next to the recliner where he'd taken it off
to rub lotion on my feet.

Brothers

after Vytautus Pliura (1951-2011)

> "The hardest thing I ever did
> was coping with the fact, growing up,
> that I was in love with my younger brother."
>   —"Thomas"

It wasn't my brother I was in love with,
or even the boys I chose to stand in his shoes, every
one of them, filling their not-my-brother mouths with
my name, their greedy arms with trophies from his dying
room. It was the idea of him I was grieving, or the idea
of something like him, something I didn't yet
have the words to say, that we could have been closer
than we were, that the only time
I remember him touching me
was the day the glass thermometer cracked mercury
across my face and I broke into the softness of
his hands. I know he must have touched me
more. I know I wanted to be touched, to share
myself with another him, or something like him,
broad but gentle, kin to me, something
like the man I was terrified to be.

Jukebox

for Jack Veasey (1955-2016)

> "I want to be a jukebox song"
> —"When I Reincarnate"

Small town anywhere a mother is
driving her son to the skating rink
because that's where the boy is
the boy that makes him feel like
a bird just out of the nest part clumsy
wing part dream of maple when every
little leap might lead to sky where
each Saturday is its own new
season where the lights will
heartbeat bright and deep
and calf will rise against calf where
a song will begin where he'll open
his mouth to sing instead a
timid moment will bloom to power
first lips like the warm wet mouthpiece
of a trumpet he'll remember
that music every first of his life

The Men We Loved

> *"Push close my lovers and take the best I possess ..."*
> —"A Song for Occupations"
> *by Walt Whitman (1819-1892)*

The men we loved, the men we had, the men we wanted.
They pass us in the streets. They are going to the gym,
to the park, to the pub, to invisible rooms on the internet.
They cast their lines of hunger for other men now.

The men we wanted who wanted nothing to do with us.
The men we hid our names from and crept away.
They are disappearing into their work, into the rest
of their lives, picking up their phones to answer
another man's voice and putting them down again.

The men we had now plough the ache of other men.
Time flips them over each other and abrades them
to the bone. These men who taught us to be bridges
on the way to somewhere else, something better.

The men we loved who wiped the disappointment
from our lips with a thumb, a tongue down a throat.
A promise to call again and the promise fulfilled.
Long before the accident, the illness, the overseas job,
a touch turned cold, the averted vision, the other man.

The men we loved, the men we had, the men we wanted.
They have done far worse than fail to miss us—
they have forgotten us. Each is slinking into a cab
with another guy and does not wave goodbye.

These men who once taught us of ourselves
crane to hear the call of new lives now, the call

that is always waiting to be answered, a boy crying
wolf, or maybe the truth this time. This truth

we leave our better selves for, only to find them again
when we least expect it, a face rising like a moon
in the night's long window, a night we are scaling with
our hearts in our mouths. Then when we reach the top
of the stairs, what luck—the moon has become a mirror.

Here

"The wildest and bloodiest is over and all is peace."
—"The Sleepers" *by Walt Whitman (1819-1892)*

Here between the country
that will not remember our love
and the sea, our clothes spill

like sand from a tilted
palm. Then we are walking
arm in arm. We are gazing

in the same, unwavering direction.
There is no need to mourn
for what we have left behind.

Look as our footprints
evaporate when we approach
the chiming of waves, waves

rising and tugging at us like joy.
This is not an ending
and time has not been

unkind. We reach the edge
of our lives. We stop in awe
of how much further we have to go.

CYRIL WONG

Take Our Cue from Time

> *"To think that we are now here and bear our part."*
> —"The Sleepers" *by Walt Whitman (1819-1892)*

Take our cue from time, the master. Learn to weigh
everything equally: hope and grief, two sides
to a partner we should love unconditionally.

Learn to love a clean kitchen, as well as the ants
around the bin like the spoor of something
left unsaid, something important.

To love the illness, the perspective earned thereafter.
To try and love death; how heroic the attempt.

Then we fail, the hours pressed too thinly.
Mirrors draw out a cry from inside the womb
of a mind swollen with terror.

Then we stop to gather the pieces again. To love
the pieces as they are, scattered all around us.

But look at how we have been tempered,
the selves that wanted and kept wanting—

they just ask for more of the same now.

Let us not give the years too much credit
for how far we have come,
for what we have become.

To love the smell of rain, the cold rain on our faces.
Love the thunder and the sleep it cracks open.

What we have now. And what will come after.

Garbage Night

after Ed Cox (1946-1992)

I get out of bed because I've forgotten again.
Every Tuesday at three-thirty a.m. the garbage
truck rumbles up our street to collect, crush,
and swallow the waste of our week.

I've also forgotten that you work weekends;
my Monday is your Friday night. So I'm surprised
when I recognize your voice from the other
balcony. You're heaving up your evening, gasping,

nearly weeping between volleys. I pause
on the fire escape, worried and reverent. I do not
wish to burden you with my presence. This
is a private ritual, and I your faithful voyeur.

In my hand a clove cigarette burns, like incense
or a votive, and I wish for us both some better way
to cleanse ourselves. That garbage you take
all week from your boss, your boyfriend, your dad.

Lord knows you can never give it all back—
not to mention all the shit you give yourself.
At last you are quiet. I toss my smoke
and send an arc of sparks out over the rail

into the dark below. You gasp—I've given
myself away, so I stay in shadow until at last
your door creaks and clicks closed. Then I
descend and drag my garbage to the street.

Wrestling with Uncle Walt

after Walt Whitman (1819-1892)

> I make a pact with you, Walt Whitman—
> I have detested you long enough.
> —Ezra Pound

I didn't like you when I was young—
that awful way you rambled on, "I am
America!" you'd cry and I'd be terrified
and look to see if neighbors watched—

the crazy uncle, singing of himself
in a dirty shirt and scuffed old boots,
Rolling on the lawn, crooning your
"Song of America," you were
inspired by your own bad breath,
sniffing your armpits, sighing, content.
On green-stained knees

you wielded a blade of grass, tried to pass
it on to me. Wisdom, you insisted—
like a maniac—more in the veins
of that one leaf than in all the writing of the world!

Your arms spread wide, you whispered
to the dirt, to sons and soldiers passed
into the earth. Blood and war nourished,
you said, grass that fed the cattle, gave
us milk, and so we all were one.
On and on like that you'd prattle and I was made

to study those long droning lines. I hated you.
Worst of all was when you hauled me to the ground
and held me down, mortified in front of friends who said,
like others have, that you were just a pervert.

I knew better, still I berated you
for loving everyone, always and in public,
for rattling my head and hairs with your dirty nails
and knuckles. I never heard your leaner lines
of restful noon-day walks and falling mating eagles,
not until I grew, and began to listen on my own

to tales of men in uniform and lilacs
in the courtyard, softer and sweeter
than the Captain's Song; of men, you'd
loved and touched with healing hands.

Now I think of you, Uncle, as I lie
with lovers on green lush lawns,
or listen in their arms to the waves
unceasingly caress the beach.

How you invited me, how I had cringed
to see you hold the hand of another man
under a dark corner table—how you swam
naked with brothers, while the widow
longingly looked on—how I am so like you.

Your path and mine treads grass and flowers,
toward a home which is always here. I know
you feed their roots, and so I look for you,
daily, beneath the soles of my road-worn boots.

DAVID GROFF

Paul Monette Has Left the Building

(1945-1995)

You ungowned yourself to show
the marvel of your swollen scrotum,
as if the jeweled egg you'd borne
from the Caucasus across the Elbe
smuggled cleverly in your pants
through Paris and past border guards
into the unsafe deposit of America
had suddenly blushed green
and grown more precious,
a scarab of remarkable powers
owned as it was by you.

Paul, you broadcast your death by inches
to governors and magazines,
performing your pinked rage,
dying no gentlemen's agreement,
no Episcopal fainting couch—
the courtier become the wizard
with his desiccant book of spells
the globe nodded slightly toward,
a ribbon wearing a hanging man,
vain, vain, and brave,
your flame so hot my face went red.

Yet when your final final assertion came,
your voice on the phone was a razor,
eerily virile—you'd forsworn all pills.
You'd write more soon, I promised—
that travel book we talked about—
No, you said, *I'm done*,
your matter all fact,
stripped for the sprint,

denying my denial,
your envoi sent.
I dropped the ball.

Epistles to Reinaldo Arenas: Invocation

(1943-1990)

I take you into my mouth, Reinaldo Arenas, mouth your praises: honeysuckle, night-blooming-jasmine, bougainvillea te invoco   sweet sickly vine that chokes off any stem it clings to   moonstroked blossom whose scent burns off come dawn   riotous purple-prosed pistil and stamen branch all thorned up.

We banter down boulevards of books. "Before night falls," you say, "I'll strip you bare. Tu piel una página para leer. Tu espalda la espina de un libro." You stroke my back, Arenas, caress each word. The alleys and sidestreets of old Nueva York are mazed library stacks. We parade paragraphs about one another. Pen in hand we scribble penis in hand we diddle we stroke each character on the page. I've absconded the past to transcribe you.

Reinaldo, mi amigo, mi amor: this is the whore your words have made. You're my skin, my spiritflesh, my holy ghost of the holy of holies of **O**. Que puta soy! I'm nearly as old as you were when you died, and I've had three soulmates in this life. The first died five minutes after I held him in my arms at Genesis Hospice. A spontaneously shattered wineglass by my nightstand   his T-cell count obliterated like crushed glass in the blood   a spear of light shot through his veins then gone by dawn. Is that how it was for you, Reinaldo? The grasp, clutch, choke of breath before morning?

My third soulmate is an enigma: all boat-liquid-fuel-ignition one moment   leaking coolant the next   but something's cracked in the engine between us   nothing works right anymore. Still, he's the taste of laughter, the curl and fin of wakes thrust up from the stern: blue water, blue horizon, all shot through with diesel fumes. It's beautiful it's cobalt it's clouded up and this is the murk I'm left with as my second soulmate stands beside me oblivious yet looking out onto the waves.

Reinaldo, mi barquito, you are the tender bridled to the boat of mi lengua. My tongue, your words: we're writing this in tandem.

Afterimage

after Walt Whitman (1819-1892)

> "No man has been photographed more than I have ..."
> —Walt Whitman, 27 July 1888

The leaf isn't gelatin, photogravure;
bark not silver, watermarked
cotton: poplar, pulse, privation.

Sugar-lift etching,
silver gelatin print, produce
a black more tangible than shadow.

Deprive the eye—drypoint—and the brain
compensates, offers engraving,
fills in the hazy outline

out of focus; constructs coherence;
gathers the gap into knowing.
Archival pigment—an image-

machine—the thought, the twig,
the dirt illuminated:
soil-nymph, water-want, aquatint-print.

And you: a body I no longer
see but in dreams, the dark
of an unexposed photograph.

Birds! Beasts! Flowers!

for D. H. Lawrence (1885-1930)

I gifted myself an ornithological retreat to the shores of the
    Mediterranean,
A tidy house with a garden, stone's throw from the pebbled
    beach.
There I meant to separate myself from the world before, or
    the world above.
In mornings, the quick-darts of hummingbirds stitched
    together the yard,
        trumpet vine to trumpet vine.
Between sips, they would wage their tiny wars, no sharing
    of the clothesline
        hung taut between poles
Until the noontime heat extinguished their grievances.

In town, I spied him as he leaned against the struts of the
    provisioner's store.
He clucked his tongue and walked beside me with a bicycle,
    offering his basket to tote the aliments
        wrapped snug in brown paper by the shopkeeper.
In the white light of afternoon, even the cobblestones
    professed heat.

His shirt was not a shirt but an afterthought, thrown on
    and open to black hairs tightly curled
        and holding their spiral.
When we came to my garden gate, he strode in like a king
    and leaned his bike against the flowering hedge.

At the pump that was meant for the garden that was not
    meant to be watered at this time of year,
        the whole town might run dry,
He lowered his head as a beast to drink.

And the water spilled over his mouth, and the water spilled
    over his face,
    its glistening unwinding in me
    a lengthening desire to drink too,
Even if there were to be no after, only this moment shared
    between two thirsts in a yard.
The one certainty seemed the anemone at his feet, purple
    petals circling black buttons
    whose unfastening might open fabric
    to the underworld.

For Constantine Cavafy

(1863-1933)

Reading your book
I see you now
again in your Alexandria,
leaning
toward the window of a shop
where the light
catches the dust and touches
the features of a young man within. Watching,
you catch sight of your reflection
mottled in the glass,
and move away,
last words of a poem
rising to your mind:
        "Later, in a happier time,
        a man just like me
        will appear, and act freely."
Sometimes,
remembering my silences,
my lost moments,
the line of burnt out candles,
I despair with you, Cavafy.
And then, sometimes,
I think: this is that happy time;
I am the man.

GAVIN GEOFFREY DILLARD

Untitled

after Walt Whitman (1819-1892)

Meditations on Uncle Walt:
bearded old scribbler on the bank of a
  creek;

a slug writes a poem on a carpet of
moss—and in this simple
 bliss, we all are set free.

Of Him I Love Day and Night

Of him I love day and night I dream'd I heard he was dead;
And I dream'd I went where they had buried him I love—
    but he was not in that place,
And I dream'd I wander'd, searching among burial-places,
    to find him;
And I found that every place was a burial-place;
The houses full of life were equally full of death, (this
    house is now;)
The streets, the shipping, the places of amusement, the
    Chicago, Boston, Philadelphia, the Mannahatta, were as
    full of the dead as of the living,
And fuller, O vastly fuller of the dead than of the living;
—And what I dream'd I will henceforth tell to every person
    and age,
And I stand henceforth bound to what I dream'd;
And now I am willing to disregard burial-places and
    dispense with them;
And if the memorials of the dead were put up indifferently
    everywhere, even in the room where I eat or sleep, I
    should be satisfied;
And if the corpse of any one I love, or if my own corpse, be
    duly render'd to powder, and pour'd in the sea, I shall be
    satisfied;
Or if it be distributed to the winds, I shall be satisfied.

CONTRIBUTORS

SHANE ALLISON's two collections include *I Remember* (Future Tense Books) and *Slut Machine* (Queer Mojo Press). His novels *You're The One I Want* and *Harm Done* are available from Strebor Books.

JEFFREY ANGLES (Translator) is a bilingual poet who writes in both Japanese and English. He currently lives and teaches in Kalamazoo, Michigan.

M. J. ARCANGELINI has had three collections of poetry published, the most recent being *Waiting for the Wind to Rise* (NightBallet Press, 2018).

GEER AUSTIN's poetry and fiction has appeared in journals, anthologies, and blogs. He is the author of *Cloverleaf*, a book of poetry from PWP Press.

STUART BARNES's *Glasshouses* (UQP, 2016) won the Thomas Shapcott Poetry Prize, and was shortlisted/commended for two other awards. Stuart was born, raised and lives in Australia. [stuartabarnes. wordpress.com] Twitter: @StuartABarnes

DAVID J. BAUMAN'S second chapbook *Angels & Adultery* was selected by Nickole Brown for the Robin Becker Chapbook Series with Seven Kitchens Press (2018). [davidjbauman.com]

JEFFERY BEAM's 25-plus works include *New Beautiful Tendons: Collected Queer Poems*, *Don't Forget Love*, and *Jonathan Williams: Lord of Orchards*, and collaborations with composers Lee Hoiby, Steven Serpa, and Tony Solitro. [jefferybeam.com]

GARY BOELHOWER's poetry collections and awards include *Naming Rites* and *Marrow, Muscle, Flight*, the Midwest Book Award, and the Foley Prize from *America* magazine.

CHARLIE BONDHUS's books of poetry include *Divining Bones* (Sundress Publications, 2018) and *All the Heat We Could Carry* (Main Street Rag, 2013). [charliebondhus.com]

BRYAN BORLAND is the founding publisher of Sibling Rivalry Press, founding editor of *Assaracus: A Journal of Gay Poetry*, and author of four books of poetry. [bryanborland.com]

JERICHO BROWN is a Guggenheim Fellow. His most recent book is *The Tradition* (Cooper Canyon Press, 2019). [jerichobrown.com]

A. J. CHILSON has been writing and performing poetry since he was a teenager. A resident of Princeton, Texas, Chilson's advice is simple: Pursue your passions.

PHILIP F. CLARK is the author of *The Carnival of Affection* (Sibling Rivalry Press, 2017). He teaches English and Poetry at City College, New York. [philipfclark.wordpress.com]

JEFFERY CONWAY's books include *Descent of the Dolls, Showgirls: The Movie in Sestinas, The Album That Changed My Life*, and *Phoebe 2002: An Essay in Verse*.

ALFRED CORN is the author of 11 books of poetry, two novels, and three collections of criticism. More information can be found on Wikipedia.

DAVID CUMMER is a long-time Minneapolis resident and has written for radio, television, and various LGBT publications. He produces the podcast *The Kinda Stories We Tell*.

PHILIP DACEY (1939-2016) is the author of 14 books of poems, including *The Ice-Cream Vigils: Last Poems*, published posthumously in November 2016 by Red Dragonfly Press. [philipdacey.com]

GAVIN GEOFFREY DILLARD is the author of a dozen books, an award-winning opera, *When Adonis Calls*, and *The Wife of Lot—a Pagan Mass*. [gavindillard.org]

PATRICK DONNELLY is the author of four books of poetry. With his spouse Stephen D. Miller, he translates classical Japanese poetry and drama. [patrickdonnellypoetry.com]

ARTHUR DURKEE is an award-winning writer, composer, visual artist, and global nomad. His poetry, short fiction, and creative nonfiction have been published worldwide. [patreon.com/ArthurDurkee]

JIM ELLEDGE's most recent books are *Bonfire of the Sodomites* (poetry) and *The Boys of Fairy Town* (Chicago gay history). He is a two-time Lambda Award winner.

JACK FRITSCHER, celebrating his 80th birthday with the 200th birthday of fellow Gemini Whitman, was first published in 1957. Sixty years of his writing is free to all at jackfritscher.com.

CONTRIBUTORS

KEITH GAREBIAN of Mississauga, Ontario, Canada has had one of his Derek Jarman poems set to music for choir and instruments by Gregory Spears. [garebian.wordpress.com]

ALEX GILDZEN is a poet and artist who lives in Palm Springs. He likes movies and chocolate.

ROBERT L. GIRON is the author of five collections of poetry. His poetry has appeared in numerous journals and anthologies, including the recent one by Latinx in the Washington, D.C. area. [robertgiron.com]

DAVID GROFF is the author of the poetry collections *Clay* and *Theory of Devolution*. [davidgroff.com]

NICHOLAS ALEXANDER HAYES is the author of *NIV: 39 & 27* (BlazeVOX), *Between* (Atropos), and *ThirdSexPot* (Beard of Bees).

TREBOR HEALEY has authored three novels, a book of poetry, and three story collections. He co-edited the anthologies *Beyond Definition* and *Queer & Catholic*. [treborhealey.com]

GREG HEWETT is the author of five poetry collections, most recently, *Blindsight* (Coffee House Press). He is Professor of English at Carleton College. [greghewettwriter.com]

SCOTT HIGHTOWER, originally from Texas, lives in Manhattan and teaches at New York University's Gallatin School of Individualized Study. [scotthightower.com]

WALTER HOLLAND is the author of three books of poetry (*A Journal of the Plague Years: Poems 1979-1992*, *Transatlantic*, and *Circuit*), and a novel (*The March*). [walterhollandwriter.com]

ANDREW HOWDLE is a retired teacher and educational consultant and an active writer who lives in Leeds, UK.

MICHAEL HYDE is the author of *What Are You Afraid Of?*, a book of stories and winner of the Katherine Anne Porter Prize in Short Fiction.

GEORGE K. ILSLEY is a Canadian author who lives in Vancouver. He has recently completed a memoir about his relationship with his father in his nineties. [thatwriter.ca]

CURRAN JEFFERY, born in 1947, a degree in history from Illinois State University, spent a lifetime making poems in Chicago, Arkansas, New Mexico, and San Diego.

JEE LEONG KOH is the author of *Steep Tea* (Carcanet), named a Best Book of the Year by UK's *Financial Times* and a Lambda Literary Award Finalist. He has published three other books of poems and a book of zuihitsu.

MICHAEL LASSELL is the author or editor of 23 books. His poetry titles include *Poems for Lost and Un-lost Boys*, *Decade Dance* (a Lambda Literary Award winner), and *A Flame for the Touch That Matters*.

TRAVIS CHI WING LAU is a postdoctoral fellow in English at UT Austin. His creative writing has appeared in *Assaracus*, *The Deaf Poets Society*, *Glass*, *Impossible Archetype*, and *Rogue Agent*. [travisclau.com]

DANIEL W.K. LEE is a Malaysian-born, ethnically Cantonese, refugee writer currently based in Seattle. He can be reached at strongplum@yahoo.com.

TIMOTHY LIU's latest book is *Luminous Debris: New & Selected Legerdemain (1992-2017)*. A reader of occult esoterica, he lives in Manhattan and Woodstock, NY. [timothyliu.net]

CHIP LIVINGSTON is the author of a novel, story collection, and two poetry collections. He teaches in the low-rez MFA program at the Institute of American Indian Arts. He lives in Montevideo, Uruguay. [chiplivingston.com]

RAYMOND LUCZAK is the author and editor of 22 books, including *A Babble of Objects* and *Flannelwood*. A ten-time Pushcart Prize nominee, he lives in Minneapolis, Minnesota. [raymondluczak.com]

JEFF MANN has published five books of poetry, two collections of essays, a memoir, three collections of short fiction, and six novels. [jeffmannauthor.com]

JAIME MANRIQUE has published novels, volumes of poems, essays, and translations in English and Spanish. He is a Distinguished Lecturer in the City College of New York.

CONTRIBUTORS

HERBERT WOODWARD MARTIN taught at the University of Dayton for three decades. He was a Fulbright Scholar in Pecs, Hungary. He performs P. L. Dunbar worldwide.

MARCOS L. MARTÍNEZ, a Lambda and Macondo Literary Fellow, has had work appear in Split This Rock and *riverSedge*. A Texas native, Marcos teaches writing at NYU-DC.

DERMOT MEAGHER is a writer and artist. He was the first openly gay judge in Massachusetts.

JORY MICKELSON is the recipient of an Academy of American Poet's Prize and a Lambda Literary Fellow in Poetry. He lives in the Pacific Northwest.

STEPHEN S. MILLS is the author of *He Do the Gay Man in Different Voices, A History of the Unmarried,* and *Not Everything Thrown Starts a Revolution.* He lives in New York City. [stephensmills.com]

MICHAEL KIESOW MOORE is the author of the poetry collection *What to Pray.* He founded the Birchbark Books Reading Series, and dances with the Ramsey's Braggarts Morris Men. [michaelkiesowmoore.org]

SP MULROY, born and raised in the rural American South, is a nationally recognized performer and an award-winning professor of poetry, music, and drama.

CHAEL NEEDLE is the Managing Editor of *A&U: America's AIDS Magazine* and the coeditor of *Art & Understanding: Literature from the First Twenty Years of A&U* along with Diane Goettel.

ERIC THOMAS NORRIS's poems have appeared in *The New English Review, Ambit, SOFTBLOW, Assaracus,* and many other journals. He lives in Portland, Oregon.

MARGARET SAYERS PEDEN (Translator) lives in Columbia, Missouri.

JAMES PENHA, a native New Yorker, lives, writes, and often sets his LGBTQ+ stories and poems in Indonesia. Penha edits *TheNewVerse. News.*

SETH PENNINGTON is Editor-in-Chief at Sibling Rivalry Press, author of *Tertulia*, and co-editor of *Assaracus* and *Joy Exhaustible*. He lives in Little Rock, Arkansas. [sethpennington.com]

FELICE PICANO is a novelist, memoirist, and playwright. He has taught at Antioch University Los Angeles and the West Hollywood Library, and lectures on film and LGBT culture. [felicepicano.net]

MARTIN POUSSON is the queer author of *Black Sheep Boy*, winner of the PEN Center USA Fiction Award, a NEA Fellowship, and finalist for the Lambda Literary Award. [martinpousson.com]

CHRISTOPHER RECORDS is a writer from Los Angeles. His short story collection *Care: Stories* is forthcoming from Inlandia Institute. Twitter: @clorecords001

WILLIAM REICHARD's sixth poetry collection, *The Night Horse: New and Selected Poems*, was published in 2018 by Bright Horse Books. [williamreichard.com]

DENNIS RHODES is the author of three poetry collections: *Spiritus Pizza and other poems*, *Entering Dennis*, and *The Letter I*. He lives in Florida.

BRUCE RILEY (Cover Artist) is a self-taught artist. Bruce lives and paints full-time in Chicago. [bruce-riley.com]

ROCCO RUSSO is currently working as a family physician and living in Litchfield County (a county without freeways) with husband Ron and labrador retriever Rozie.

ROBERTO F. SANTIAGO's debut, *Angel Park*, was a Lambda Literary finalist. He lives in San Francisco with a fiction writer and black cat that never stops biting him. [therfsantiago.com]

GERARD SARNAT MD has won prizes, and been nominated for Pushcarts and Best of the Net Awards. Gerry's authored four collections and is widely published. [gerardsarnat.com]

P. C. SCEARCE is a disabled queer poet from Danville, Virginia who lives in D.C. He was a 1994 graduate of Averett University and an MFA candidate in GMU's Poetry program.

CONTRIBUTORS

JAMES SCHWARTZ is a poet, slam performer, writer, and author of four poetry collections including *The Literary Party: Growing Up Gay and Amish in America* and *Punatic*. [literaryparty.blogspot.com]

DAVIS G. SEE is a gay writer and "Kanadian of the north." He was a poetry editor for The Bolo Tie Collective's second and third anthologies. "Comrade" is his first published poem.

GREGG SHAPIRO is the author of *Fifty Degrees* (Seven Kitchens), *How to Whistle* (Lethe Press), *Lincoln Avenue* (Squares & Rebels), *GREGG SHAPIRO: 77* (Souvenir Spoon Press), and *Protection* (Gival Press).

BEN SHIELDS is a writer, editor, and journalist. His work has appeared in *The Paris Review*, *Bookforum*, *Hyperallergic*, and others. He lives in New York.

ALLEN SMITH, a double-leg amputee, lives in Alexandria, Virginia, with his partner of 25 years. His work appears in *Crucible*, *Broad River Review*, and *My Diva*.

MICHAEL D. SNEDIKER is the author of *The New York Editions*, *The Apartment of Tragic Appliances*, and *Queer Optimism: Lyric Personhood and Other Felicitous Persuasions*.

FREDERICK SPEERS is the author of *So Far Afield*, a finalist for the Lambda Award for Gay Poetry. He lives in Denver with his husband. [frederickspeers.com]

MALCOLM STUHLMILLER graduated from the University of Minnesota. He is busily retired on the North Shore of Lake Superior with his husband of 37 years.

MUTSUO TAKAHASHI has, since the 1960s, been Japan's most prominent gay poet. His most famous homoerotic poetry appears in the collection *Poems of a Penisist*.

ATSUSUKE TANAKA lives in Kyoto, Japan where he is a math teacher by day and an experimental, postmodern poet by night.

GUY TERRELL co-wrote *The Fourth Branch of Government: We the People* plus *A Short History of Richmond*, and published poems in *Tar River Poetry Review* and *Streetlight*.

ULYSSES TETU is a white, Minnesotan, bisexual Bear-to-be who writes pithy poetry for e-journals like *Kingdoms in the Wild* and *Lahar Berlin*. [busyliz.weebly.com]

JOHN WHITTIER TREAT is a writer in Seattle. His short story, "The Pond," was awarded the 2018 Christopher Hewitt Prize for Fiction by *A&U Magazine*. [johntreat.com]

DAVID TRINIDAD's most recent collection of poetry is *Swinging on a Star* (Turtle Point Press, 2017). He is a Professor of Poetry at Columbia College Chicago.

MARK WARD is the author of *Circumference* (Finishing Line Press, 2018) and founding editor of *Impossible Archetype*, a journal of LGBTQ+ poetry. [astintinyourspotlight.wordpress.com]

EDMUND WHITE has received the PEN/Bellow Award for Lifetime Achievement. He has written novels, memoirs, travel books, biographies—and about ten poems! [edmundwhite.com]

WALT WHITMAN (1819-1892) was an American poet who eventually changed the world of literature with the self-publication of *Leaves of Grass* in 1855. [whitmanarchive.org]

SCOTT WIGGERMAN is the author of *Leaf and Beak: Sonnets, Presence,* and *Vegetables and Other Relationships*; and the editor of others, including the best-selling *Wingbeats*. [swig.tripod.com]

JIM WISE's poetry has been featured in such venues as *The Gay & Lesbian Review, RFD, So It Goes, The Best American Non-Required Reading,* and *Odin's Gift*.

CYRIL WONG is a poet from Singapore. His last collection was *The Lover's Inventory*, which received the Singapore Literature Prize in 2016.

IAN YOUNG is the author of several poetry collections including *Year of the Quiet Sun, Common-or-Garden Gods,* and *Sex Magick*. His most recent book is *London Skin & Bones: The Finsbury Park Stories* (Squares & Rebels). He lives in Toronto.

ACKNOWLEDGMENTS

The following poems were previously published (and in a few cases revised for this anthology):

Shane Allison: "This is Where Frank O'Hara Lives," Allison's *Slut Machine* (Queer Mojo).

David J. Bauman: "Wrestling with Uncle Walt," Bauman's *Dad Poet Blog*.

Jeffrey Beam: "Physical Love," "That Night," and "A Welcome to the Black Sun," Beam's *The New Beautiful Tendons: Collected Queer Poems 1969-2012* (Spuyten Duyvil/Triton Press); "Sebastian at Siege," Beam's *The Fountain* (North Carolina Wesleyan College Press).

Gary Boelhower: "Upon Waking," Boelhower's *Marrow, Muscle, Flight: Poems* (Wildwood River Press).

Charlie Bondhus: "New York School," Bondhus's *How the Boy Might See It* (Jane's Boy Press).

Jericho Brown: "After Essex Hemphill," *Adroit*; "Duplex," *American Poetry Review*; "Of My Fury," *Tin House*; "Token," *The Paris Review*.

Jeffery Conway: "Dead Poet," *MiPOesias Revista Literaria*.

Alfred Corn: "The Bridge, Palm Sunday 1973," Corn's *All Roads at Once* (Viking Press).

Philip Dacey: "Walt and Joe," *The Hopkins Review*.

Patrick Donnelly: "Lorca's Lips," *American Poetry Review*.

Jim Elledge: "Lullaby," *Luna Luna*; "TV Guide," *Good Men Project*.

Keith Garebian: "Queer Artist Haiku," *Blue: The Derek Jarman Poems* (Signature Editions).

Alex Gildzen: "Alone in Cleveland," Gildzen's *Cleveland: Point B in Ohio Triangle* (Crisis Chronicles Press); "Body Parts," Gildzen's *Son of Hollywood* (NightBallet Press).

David Groff: "Paul Monette Has Left the Building," Groff's *Clay* (Trio House Press).

Trebor Healey: "A Nightclub South of Market," *Priapus*.

Scott Hightower: "April 11, 1861, Arrowhead," Hightower's *Natural Trouble* (Fordham University Press); "Era Un Maricón" and One Arm," Hightower's *Self-evident* (Barrow Street Books).

Curran Jeffery: "Robust Democracy," Jeffery's *Holding Hands with Reality* (Author House).

Daniel W.K. Lee: "La Cocina," *Narcolepsy Arms*; "The Rain," Robert L. Giron's *Poetic Voices Without Borders* (Gival Press).

Chip Livingston: "I Remember Joe Brainard's Cock Pics," *Punctuate Magazine*; "Long Island Jitney Interlude," *The Rumpus*.

Jeff Mann: "New Orleans Ode," *Polari Journal*; "Training the Enemy," *Pine Mountain Sand & Gravel*.

Marcos L. Martinez: "Epistles to Reinaldo Arenas: Invocation," *HIV +/- Here and Now*.

ACKNOWLEDGMENTS

Jory Mickelson: "Dear Federico," *Superstition Review*; "Faith" (originally titled "After"), *Faultline Journal of Arts and Letters*.

Chael Needle: "Skimming the Spine," *The Adirondack Review*.

James Penha: "Rimbaud's Revisions," Penha's *No Bones to Carry: Poems* (New Sins Press).

Rocco Russo: "what makes a poem gay?", *Chopper*.

Mutsuo Takahashi: "Love Poetry and the Reader," entitled "Koi no shi to yomu hito," appeared in Japanese for Takahashi's *Tsui kinō no koto* (*Only Yesterday*) (Shichōsha); "With Twig in Hand," entitled "Koeda o motte," appeared in Japanese for Takahashi's *Koeda o motte* (*With Twig in Hand*) (Shoshi Yamada).

Atsusuke Tanaka: "Get Your Filthy Hands Off My Desert" appeared in Japanese in *Shi no renshū*.

David Trinidad: "James Schuyler" and "To Tim Dlugos," Trinidad's *Dear Prudence: New and Selected Poems* (Turtle Point Press); "Joe," Trinidad's *Notes on a Past Life* (BlazeVOX [books]).

Scott Wiggerman: "Hart Crane: A Cento," *The Unlost Journal*.

Cyril Wong: "Here," "The Men We Loved," and "Take Our Cue from Time" Wong's *Tilting Our Plates to Catch the Light* (Math Paper Press).

Ian Young: "For Constantine Cavafy," *Gay News*.

Also Available from Squares & Rebels

Some of us grow up as squares, and some of us grow up as rebels. Sometimes it's the other way around. More so when we grow up feeling different. And sometimes, when we're done with living with our parents, we rebel and surprise ourselves in the most shocking ways.

In 2012, Squares & Rebels was created by Handtype Press to bring out anthologies initially about the LGBT experience in the Midwest. With the publication of *QDA: A Queer Disability Anthology*, however, S&R has expanded its focus to include books that explore the queer and/or disability experience regardless of one's region of origin.

Our titles, starting with the most recent, follow.

We will always appreciate your purchases of our books via squaresandrebels.com. Thank you!